THE SECRET OF LOVE

ALSO BY HAROLD KLEMP

MAHANTA

This book has been authored by and published under the supervision of the Mahanta, the Living ECK Master, Sri Harold Klemp. It is the Word of ECK.

THE SECRET OF LOVE

HAROLD KLEMP

MAHANTA TRANSCRIPTS
BOOK 14

ECKANKAR
Minneapolis, MN

The Secret of Love, Mahanta Transcripts, Book 14

Copyright © 1996 ECKANKAR

Printed in U.S.A.

Compiled by Mary Carroll Moore
Edited by Joan Klemp and Anthony Moore
Text illustrations by Valerie Taglieri and Ron Wennekes
Text photo (page xii) by Bernard Chouet
Back cover photo by Robert Huntley

Library of Congress Cataloging-in-Publication Data

Klemp, Harold.
    The secret of love / Harold Klemp.
        p. cm. — (Mahanta transcripts ; bk. 14)
    Includes index.
    ISBN 1-57043-114-0 (perfect bound)
    1. Eckankar (Organization)—Doctrines. 2. Spiritual life—
Eckankar (Organization) I. Title. II. Series: Klemp, Harold.
Mahanta Transcripts ; bk. 14.
BP605.E3K5648 1996
299'.93—dc20   96-41518
                                                CIP

♾ The paper used in this publication meets the minimum requirements of the American National Standard for Information Sciences—Permanence of Paper for Printed Library Materials, ANSI Z39.48-1984.

CONTENTS

FOREWORD

The teachings of ECK define the nature of Soul. You are Soul, a particle of God sent into the worlds (including earth) to gain spiritual experience.

The goal in ECK is spiritual freedom in this lifetime, after which you become a Co-worker with God, both here and in the next world. Karma and reincarnation are primary beliefs.

Key to the ECK teachings is the Mahanta, the Living ECK Master. He has the special ability to act as both the Inner and Outer Master for ECK students. He is the prophet of Eckankar, given respect but not worship. He teaches the sacred name of God, HU, which lifts you spiritually into the Light and Sound of God, the ECK (Holy Spirit). Purified by the practice of the Spiritual Exercises of ECK, you are then able to accept the full love of God in this lifetime.

Sri Harold Klemp is the Mahanta, the Living ECK Master. He has written many books, discourses, and articles about the spiritual life. Many of his public talks are available on audio- and video-cassette. His teachings uplift people and help them recognize and understand their own experiences in the Light and Sound of God.

The Secret of Love, Mahanta Transcripts, Book 14, contains his talks from 1994–95. May they help you find love, wisdom, and spiritual freedom.

Sri Harold Klemp, the Mahanta, the Living ECK Master helps individuals in their spiritual search for the secret of love.

1
SUNSHINE AND SPARKLE

*S*ome friends of ours have two cockatiels. Beautiful birds about eight
inches tall. The couple got them as
little birds that hadn't yet learned any
expressions or phrases from other people. So the
words they know are what they've learned at home.

The owners taught them one- or two-word phrases.
But the male bird, Sunshine, began putting words
together in his own way, and they made sense.

Some people feel that humans are the highest
creation of God. It flatters us to think so highly of
ourselves. And yet as we look at the world today, any
thinking person would have doubts about the great
spiritual nature of the human race. You'd have to say
that the human race has a long ways to go. It has
a long ways to go in understanding love and divine
wisdom.

But these two cockatiels, Sunshine and Sparkle,
are—how can I say it?—a good couple. Sunshine
does all the talking. The owners suspect Sparkle is
more intelligent even though she doesn't talk. In
most relationships, this is the case. One of the couple
does a lot of talking. The other one is silent and is
probably more intelligent.

I know that's true at home. My wife doesn't talk very much.

These birds learned several expressions. The owners taught them how to say, "Kiss, kiss." Sometimes they would say, "I love you." And at other times, "Sweet baby." Pretty little things to teach birds who are going to repeat everything you say — especially when someone comes over unexpectedly and the bird repeats some phrases that you wished he hadn't.

Children do the same thing. Often you can tell what parents think by what their children say in school. If parents have prejudices, children will act them out. If you confront these parents with what their children have said and done, the parents often become very angry. "How can you accuse my child of saying and doing those things?" Actually everyone knows that the parents are doing the same sort of thing. I'm talking of younger children before they come under the influence of their peers.

One day Sunshine put some of the phrases together. He ran after Sparkle, came up behind her, and said, "I love you, sweet baby." Then he made a kissing noise. She put up with it. But sometimes she gets tired of it; she just turns her back and walks away from him. There's poor Sunshine, all full of this love. So he goes up to a mirror. And he looks in the mirror and says, "Hello, sweet baby. I love you."

When Sparkle sees him doing this to the mirror, she thinks it's a waste of endearments and she runs back to him. Then he can say his sweet nothings to her.

WE ARE SOUL

People think that they have a soul. They say very proudly, "I have a soul." But we in ECK say, "I am

Soul." This is probably the most important difference between us and other people. "I have a soul" is possessive, like "I can own Soul." You can't own Soul because you are Soul. You are a spark of God. You are divine Light and Sound put together in a form called Soul. And this Soul inhabits a physical body—sometimes a human body, but sometimes an animal body or a bird body.

You can't own Soul because you are Soul. You are a spark of God.

In the Middle Ages, the Catholic Church was so sure that we were the center of the universe. Why not? We had a holy scripture that said God made man in His likeness. Therefore, the universe must revolve around earth. Why? Because mankind is the jewel—the crowning jewel—of creation, of course.

It's such a flattering self-image. You wonder how the human race can take a step without tripping. The fact is, it can't.

When you have such a high opinion of yourself, you find you're always tripping and falling down. And so does the human race.

Soul comes in many forms, including birds. Scientists do their studies, and they're constantly surprised when birds behave the way humans do. They can have logical behavior, and they can learn from their mistakes.

BIRD TRICKS

Sunshine, the talkative one, noticed that the man of the house would always jump up when the phone rang. Pretty soon, Sunshine learned how to imitate the sound of a telephone ringing.

The man would hear the phone ring. He would run to answer the phone, and nobody would be there. Then he'd look around the room, and in his birdcage, Sunshine was ringing. Which of course meant, "Come over. Pick me up. I want love." So the man would go over and give Sunshine some attention.

These birds are like children. Bedtime comes, and they think of any excuse to put it off, like children who say, "Dad, I really like the stories you read. Could you read me a story?"

That's nice flattery. You say, "OK, I'll read you a story." The child is so interested. I know this from my own experience. They say, "Boy, that was good. Is there time for just one more?" So you read another story.

Sunshine has his own trick. When it gets near bedtime, he starts making the ringing sound. Finally it comes time to put the cloth over the cage, to put the birds in a dark place so they can get some sleep.

When the morning comes, Sunshine is there to greet the person who pulls the cloth off the cage. When the woman of the house takes the cloth off, he's very sweet. He says, "I love you." When the man comes, he says, "Hello?" That's because he's the one who picks up the phone when Sunshine makes the ringing sound. It's hard on the self-esteem of the gentleman of the house.

SAFE HAVEN

There are also two cats in the house. One is an adult cat, a very definite threat to the birds. When that cat is near the cage, the birds will squawk in warning. They forget to talk. Even Sunshine won't talk. He just squawks. But when the young cat comes near, things are different. It's still at that tender age where Sunshine thinks there is time to convince the young cat about being a good person, learning the right way—befriending birds, for instance, instead of having them for dinner.

So when the young cat comes up to the cage,

Sunshine says, "Are you my sweet baby? Are you my sweet baby?" The cat, of course, has no idea what this all means, but Sunshine is trying to convert him.

Sometimes the day has been rough. The man of the house comes home from work and listens to the news, hearing about all the unrest and political corruption around the world. He says it's just good to come home to their safe little haven; greet the dogs, the cats, and the cockatiels; and just settle down and rest for the evening.

It's their shelter. It's the place where they share love, where they can get themselves together and gain the strength to face tomorrow.

SOUL'S PURPOSE IN THIS WORLD

Soul's whole purpose for being in this world is to find divine love.

Soul's whole purpose for being in this world is to find divine love. People come to the teachings of ECK for a number of reasons. Some come for the phenomenal things, like the gift of prophecy. They want to learn Soul Travel, which is a spiritual art. Or they want the gift of healing.

But those who are farther ahead spiritually come to ECK with the desire to find love, divine love. In fact, before they find ECK, they have often asked, "Show me how to find love." And then they find it in ECK.

This is not to say that people in other paths don't do the same thing in their particular religion. God has established all religions because each religion serves a purpose. Each religion fills the needs of a certain group of Souls. And within each religion, there are those who are more advanced spiritually and those who are just starting out on the spiritual path.

This accounts for the wide range of behavior in people. Just because someone is a Christian is no guarantee that person will be an ethical and morally upright person. And just because a person is an ECKist offers no similar guarantee. In ECK, we also have people who are far advanced spiritually and others who are just beginning the spiritual path. But for whatever reason a person chooses a certain religion, it answers that Soul's spiritual needs of the day. And this day may last a lifetime; it may last several lifetimes. It may last a year or only a week.

We are all where we belong in our state of consciousness.

The point is, we are all where we belong in our state of consciousness.

CHANGE OF PLANS

The World Series got canceled this year. Those of you in the United States are familiar with the baseball strike. Those from other countries couldn't care less. You've got your own sports. But we've had a baseball strike here that canceled the World Series—which usually comes right around the time of the ECK Worldwide Seminar.

People are always trying to decide, Can they catch the game before they come down to the ECK talks? No conflict this year.

As a result of the strike, people put more attention on other baseball and softball leagues. Since the major leagues weren't playing, they put their attention on their home games, their children's games.

One of the ECK members remembered all the times I'd talked about my daughter getting interested in softball. She was a tiny tot back then—eight or nine years old.

ARE WE MOVING AHEAD?

Now she's just turned twenty-one. Time goes so fast. One day, they're five. Then they're nine. And then suddenly, they're twenty-one. At the age of fourteen, she was saying she couldn't wait for her fifteenth birthday because then she'd be a grown woman. You want to laugh when you hear somebody just starting in the teen years saying, "Well, I'm now a full-grown adult." When you get to be about my age, in the fifties, you look back and say, "I knew so much then. And now there's so much more to know than I could even begin to know. What a great life."

But when you're that young, you think you know it all. When you get older—if you have any sense at all, if life has beaten you around any bit at all—you just say, "I'm grateful for what I have."

You find that love comes in small ways and small places. And those ways and places are just as precious as when love comes in a big wave.

Life is a series of these experiences all put together: the big, the little, the important, the unimportant. And so we go through this journey of Soul, becoming more godlike in wisdom and in divine love— that is, of course, if we are moving forward spiritually.

You find that love comes in small ways and small places.

SOFTBALL LESSONS

An ECKist father had a daughter who was just getting interested in softball. She'd never played before. So he was pretty much in the role of the ECK Masters who find people who want to take another step spiritually. This father wondered, *How do I show her? How do I let her develop herself to be the best she can be?* Because the coach can't go on the field and play first base or pitch or do any of those other things in a game. The players have to do that themselves.

The daughter joined a new softball team in a very competitive league. It was an expansion team. None of the girls had ever played before. The first year, they lost all their games—fifteen or sixteen. Some of the scores were as bad as forty-eight to three, thirty-seven to three. The father found it very hard to explain to his daughter why the other team would have to overdo it like that. Thirty-seven to three is a terrible score.

In the first year, the team lost every game. The second year, the team won two games out of fifteen or sixteen. The third year arrived. Another expansion team joined the circuit, and they were going to play that team twice.

So the coach—the father of this girl—figured, "Well, another expansion team has got to be worse than our team. So maybe we can pick up two more wins. Maybe we'll get four wins for the season, and we'll be doing well."

But his daughter was very self-disciplined. She enjoyed playing softball. It's the same if you're going to walk a spiritual path or join a religion, you should enjoy it. You put yourself into it—whether you're a Catholic or a Lutheran or a Pentecostal or an ECKist. If you're going to be on the team, be a good team member. Go out and practice. Do whatever your church says is the right thing to do for your religion to grow spiritually.

Whenever the sun was shining, his daughter would drag him outside twice a day for practice. He knew she had become a very good player—many times better than she had been the year before. But he wasn't so sure about her teammates.

The season started off very well. Before they knew it, they had a record of eight wins, no defeats.

They were going to play last year's champions in the final game of the season. If they tied or won this game, they would tie for first place. If they lost, the team would get second place. It was still a very good record considering this was only their third year.

So the game started, and it was a low-scoring game. After a few innings, the score was one to nothing in favor of their opponents. Then his daughter came up to bat. And she hit a ball very deep into the outfield.

FULFILLING YOUR DESTINY

As soon as the ball got out there, the girl on the other team who was playing outfield threw up her hands — a signal to the umpire which said, "The ball has rolled under the fence." Instead of a home run, this would mean the daughter would have to go back to second base.

So the father came out. He was the coach. He discussed it with the umpire. "That ball wasn't anywhere near the fence," the father said. "And if it rolled under the fence, how could the outfielder pick the ball up? If it had been on the other side of the fence, she couldn't have reached it. She wasn't even close to it."

But the umpire said, "She threw up her hands, and that automatically makes it a ground-rule double."

The players of the opposing team had told them that their coach had a standing rule that whenever a ball got past one of the outfielders and was near the fence, they were to cheat and throw up their hands and act as if it were under the fence.

The coach didn't like this. But he tried to show the same sense of spiritual balance that all the girls on his daughter's team did. He didn't get upset. And he noticed that the girls played like ECK Masters.

They kept calm no matter what befell them, no matter how badly a break went against them. They never got upset. And the reason they didn't get upset: They had started at the bottom two years ago, and they knew all the hardships that could happen in a game. They had seen everything. They had been at the very bottom, and they had worked their way up to the top.

In the final inning the daughter's team was up to bat last. Two players had struck out already, so there was only one out to go.

His daughter came up to bat. He hoped she would have just one more hit in her, but she hit the ball very weakly. It just dribbled past the first baseman, but it got her on base. The next player also hit a weak ball, but she also got on base. And then, against all odds, the third girl hit the ball hard, deep into center field, and they scored two runs. The team won the game and tied for the championship.

The father realized that if he had become upset, he might have changed the destiny of these girls who had worked so hard to achieve the cochampionship themselves.

He remembered something from *Stranger by the River* by Paul Twitchell. It said, "Do not partake of the evil of another." So when the other coach had cheated them, this coach had kept his temper. He let the game play out on the field, and the girls won. They had fulfilled their own destiny.

Sometimes it takes a great amount of self-discipline and love to let events play themselves out and not get in our own way.

Sometimes it takes a great amount of self-discipline and love to let events play themselves out and not get in our own way. Often we get in our own way by displays of anger, temper, greed, or vanity. We hurt ourselves spiritually. We try to move ahead at the expense of others. And then we're surprised when life slaps us in the face and sets us back two steps for every step we've taken.

Through all this, we are speaking of the ECK. This is our name for Divine Spirit, the Holy Spirit, the Holy Ghost, the Comforter—whatever term you're used to. Sometimes It's known as the Audible Life Stream, but for our purposes, we often just speak of Divine Spirit, or the ECK.

UNEXPECTED HELP FROM ECK

A young mother fell and hurt her foot badly. She went to the emergency room and the doctors X-rayed her foot. They said, "Your foot's OK. Nothing wrong with it. Here are some crutches. It's going to hurt a little while, and then it will heal and you'll be OK in a couple of days."

So she hobbled out of the emergency room on her crutches and went home. But after three weeks, she still couldn't walk. Her personal doctor had also said, "It's just a bruise. It's going to take three to four weeks to heal," and sent her home.

Here the doctors were telling her that she was OK, but she couldn't walk.

I had the same experience. I went to doctors and said, "I'm having certain problems." And they gave me all kinds of checkups, then they said, "Clean bill of health." And then like this person, I asked, "Well, if my foot's OK, why can't I walk?"

The woman asked the Mahanta, the spiritual guide in Eckankar, "What is the matter? Why can't I get help?" And she asked for help. Within an hour, the doorbell rang.

She went to the door, and a young man outside introduced himself. He said, "Hi. I'm your new neighbor." He said he was setting up a medical practice and just wanted to introduce himself.

She said, "What field are you in?"

He said, "I'm a podiatrist, a foot specialist." So she invited him in, of course.

She showed him her foot. He said, "Get me the X rays from the emergency room. I'll look at them and let you know."

When he read them, he saw that her foot was fractured. "Because it's been this way for three weeks, you're going to have to have an operation," he told her. He referred her to some other doctors to take care of this quickly. He said, "If you don't have this operation, you'll never walk again."

The woman took his advice and went to these particular doctors who were very good. As she was lying on the operating table, she asked them all to sing HU as they put her to sleep. I guess you get your last request.

When she woke up, the pain was excruciating. So they gave her injections of morphine. The morphine did no good. The pain was still there.

In desperation, the woman called out, "Mahanta." It's the name of the spiritual guide in Eckankar, the inner part of myself. It's really Divine Spirit that heals. I don't do the healing. But the Mahanta is a personal form that people can relate to, and in this way, the healing occurs through the Inner Master.

As she said this name, she found the pain went away. When it came back, she sang Mahanta again, and the pain receded. In this way she was able to get through the first hours after her operation.

Sometimes divine love brings not only healing but protection.

DIVINE PROTECTION IN AFRICA

Sometimes divine love brings not only healing but protection. Another member of Eckankar is in the healing profession in Nigeria and was visiting a health clinic in one area, then he was going to go to Lagos. The day before the journey, he had his car looked over.

The journey was to be along an expressway which was a clear, easy drive, and the man had no concerns about the trip. Until he picked up the car. After he started the engine, it suddenly stopped.

So the man got out of the car and looked under the hood. Another man ran up and said, "Look! There's oil spilling out from under there." The ECKist saw that the mechanic who had been checking the engine hadn't put the pieces back together correctly, and oil was spilling out of the engine.

He called the mechanic over. The mechanic fixed the leak and apologized profusely for the mistake. And then this health worker got in the car and began to drive on the expressway again. But the car still lurched and jerked, and he couldn't figure out why.

So he pulled off the expressway and drove back to the mechanic's shop, the car still jerking and sputtering. The mechanic was very surprised to see him again. He did some work with the carburetor and fixed the contact points. "Now it's OK," the mechanic said. "The car's tuned, and you can go."

Divine Spirit has Its own hand in our affairs to save us from trouble of a more serious kind.

But this time, as the man tried to get to the expressway, he found the car was locked in first gear. This was the third thing that had gone wrong after the car was looked over by a reputable mechanic. At this point, he was wondering, *How reputable is this mechanic?* But sometimes Divine Spirit has Its own hand in our affairs to save us from trouble of a more serious kind.

So again, the ECKist called up the mechanic. The mechanic again took the car into the shop and looked it over.

A very odd thing had happened. A cable that goes to the speedometer had somehow gotten wrapped around a part of the shifting mechanism, locking the car in first gear. This had never happened before. And so the ECKist waited till the car was fixed. There was still time to get to Lagos but the man said, "No, the Mahanta is trying to tell me not to make this journey today." And so he stayed home.

A very wise man. He had divine wisdom.

GIFT OF RANDOMITY

The next day, he got up early, jumped into his car, and headed down the expressway. The trip went just as smoothly as could be—until he came to a certain place. Suddenly, there was a loud buzzing sound in his ear and a voice said, "Look off to the side."

This is the Voice of God in Its highest form, expressing Itself to Soul.

This buzzing sound is one of the many sounds of Divine Spirit when It's coming through directly. Sometimes, the music can be like an orchestra or like the ringing of bells in the distance. This is the Voice of God in Its highest form, expressing Itself to Soul.

When he looked off to the side of the road, he saw a truck and a car that had been in a huge wreck the day before. The car was just a tangled mass of steel. And the ECKist said, "Mahanta, what does this mean?"

"The destiny of this accident was to have involved three vehicles," the Inner Master told him. "Yours was the third one."

The ECKist then realized that his car's extraordinary problems were Divine Spirit's way of warning him not to make the trip the day before. And wisely, he had listened. He did not become angry. He didn't scold the mechanic or say, "I've got to keep on schedule. I've got to go anyway." He didn't do any of that.

He had the wisdom to look at outer events and then change his plans.

As Soul goes farther on the path to God, It develops the gift of randomity, which means being able to move here, there, or anywhere. To other people, it looks like a random walk. But to the individual under the guidance of Divine Spirit, it's walking the path of Light and Sound, the Light and Sound of God.

MANY BLESSINGS

We're moving from one spiritual year to the next— from the Year of Giving to a Year of Thanksgiving— a very natural transition. And sometimes in giving, we give so much that there's almost no more to give.

And so when we come to the end of a year with such a theme as giving, we are thankful to have made it. There's a lot of thanksgiving inside us just for making it into the new spiritual year of ECK. I know this is true for some of you, and it's certainly true for me.

A businessman was in Istanbul, waiting at the airport for a direct flight to Zurich, Switzerland. As he sat in the waiting room, he saw one of the airline attendants come in with a very old woman. This old woman seemed not to have traveled very often. She was confused by the check-in process, the passport control, and the security check.

The ECKist had a nudge from the Mahanta to go up to her and talk. She spoke the same Swiss dialect that he spoke, so they talked a little bit.

She said she had been visiting her son in southern Turkey. The son was in the tourist business, but she had missed her direct flight from there to Zurich, and so she had to come to Istanbul and then try to make connections. And she was having just a terrible time getting a flight. When it came time for boarding, the

As Soul goes farther on the path to God, It develops the gift of randomity, which means being able to move here, there, or anywhere.

woman finally got a seat in coach.

The businessman realized how many blessings he had received in ECK over all these years. So he went up to the woman and said, "If you like, you could have my seat in business class. The cabin crew is very attentive, the food is good, and the seats are wider. You'll enjoy the flight more." The woman was happy to switch seats with him.

The businessman went back to the coach section of the plane to read his newspapers and eat the food that the rest of us generally eat. He had good memories, though, and good thoughts of his family waiting for him when he got home.

When love is on the field, fear must retreat.

LOVE MAKES FEAR RETREAT

When the plane landed in Zurich, the woman came up to him. She was very grateful for the gift he had given her. And he realized then how happy he was too. By giving, he had received. And in his line of business, he said, there is a lot of tension, a lot of fear, and he realizes that by giving of himself when he travels like this, it diminishes that fear.

Why? Because when he gives of himself to someone else in need, it releases the divine love in the heart. And when love is on the field, fear must retreat.

This is why it's good, when you are afraid, to find a way to give to someone else. Maybe this will help you overcome your fear. Maybe it will help you through the dark hour until the sun comes up.

RELYING ON THE MAHANTA

Another person came to this country seeking political asylum, and he was put into detention until the immigration officials could hear his case. Many of the people in the detention center had friends or relatives or money to hire attorneys to help hurry their cases through. The man didn't have any money, friends, or relatives. "That's going to make it very hard for you," the others told him. But he didn't know what else to do.

As time passed, he began to wonder what would happen to him. Many of the people in the detention building were not granted political asylum and were sent back to their homeland. The man became afraid.

So he asked in contemplation, "Mahanta, are you with me? Are you with me still?" No answer.

In his next contemplation, he asked the same question. No answer. Then he asked a third time. As he sat in contemplation, a white light grew inside his Spiritual Eye, and it grew in its brightness and brilliance until it had encompassed him completely. As this light engulfed him, he had a sense of joy and happiness, and there in the spiritual worlds he found himself clapping his hands in joy. Then he awoke. He was back in the physical body.

Shortly after that, his case went through immigration without a hitch. It was very smooth and very fast.

Afterward the man wrote me. He often wonders about those people who finally find ECK and then leave it. Have they never been alone? Have they never been without friends or family, without money, or without hope? Have they never been thrown upon the mercies of life? Have they never had to rely totally upon the Mahanta?

As this light engulfed him, he had a sense of joy and happiness, and there in the spiritual worlds he found himself clapping his hands in joy.

A BRIGHT WHITE LIGHT

A couple of weeks ago I had to mail an express package. My wife went with me. The express-mail company was in a mall, one of many businesses there. We had finished our business, made copies, and mailed the package. My wife wondered whether we should walk out the side door or down the center of the mall.

Generally I ask Divine Spirit—even in little things.

Generally I ask Divine Spirit—even in little things. Divine Spirit said, "Go down the center of the mall, right down the main aisle."

Directly outside the express-mail company, a craft fair was set up—all kinds of tables where people were selling their crafts, beads and jewelry, scarves, and all kinds of different things. The first table we saw had a woman seated behind it. She had the most beautiful white aura, like a bright lightbulb in a dark hall.

I just stood there for a minute, making believe I was looking at what she had for sale. She suddenly looked at me very strangely and said, "I know you."

I didn't say anything. I just stood there because she had this pretty white aura. She said again, "I know you."

I said, "Who?" I wasn't going to make it real easy, you know.

She said, "You're Harold."

I said, "Yes."

She wasn't a member of Eckankar. She had met Paul Twitchell years ago under extraordinary circumstances. And we've met each other on the spiritual planes. As we talked about one thing or another, she said, "I've prayed for this." For her, it was important to meet someone who is working for Divine Spirit as she is.

I was just standing there enjoying the white light from her aura, which I didn't tell her about. She's not a member of ECK, but she can see the light in other people.

She said she watched the videos of my seminar talks; they're on television in the Minneapolis area each Friday night.

Sometimes I meet people years before they join Eckankar. Eventually it gets through the thick skull of the human consciousness that these people belong in ECK. Life finally teaches them this. Then they see my picture or the picture of one of the other ECK Masters and they say, "Why, that's my guide. Since I was a child." And they're surprised to find that these people are all from the family of ECK.

I meet people years before they join Eckankar.

This woman gave me a gift, a tape of a Lakota woman singing her songs of worship. And so I accepted her gift. Sometimes I say, "No, I couldn't take the gift." But this was a gift of the heart, and I just accepted it. Then later, I sent her something that I thought would be useful to her.

A Day of Thanksgiving

As my wife and I drove back into Minneapolis, at the first red light I looked to the left over a field and a hill. I said to my wife, "Look. Two hawks." And as we sat there at the light, the two hawks flew over the intersection right over our car and went in a nice circle as we were watching. And then the light turned green. It was just a very good connection with the Soul we had just met in the mall who had given us this gift of the spiritual songs of a Lakota woman.

So for me, it was a day of thanksgiving—and maybe it was for her.

Remember the two cockatiels—Sunshine and Sparkle. If we are truly aware of the hand of the Divine Spirit in our daily lives, we would feel like Sunshine and Sparkle more often. We would carry this attitude with us in our daily lives.

We would learn to put two and two together spiritually, to put the spiritual laws together into spiritual order so that they will work for us in our own lives.

ECK Worldwide Seminar, Atlanta, Georgia,
Friday, October 21, 1994

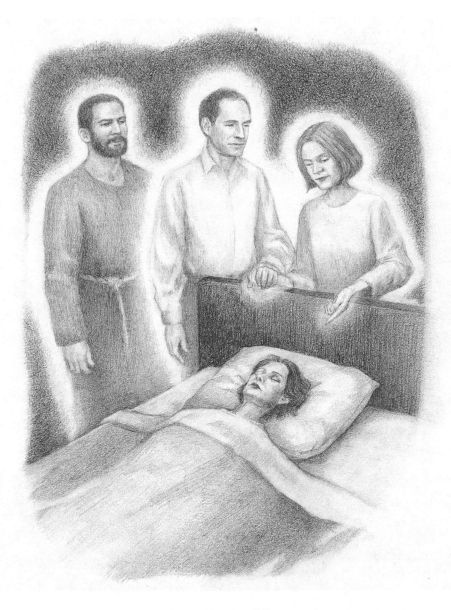

"I have a daughter. So for that reason, I would like to go back," the woman said. The ECK Master said to her, "All right. You have earned the right of choice."

2

THE RIGHT OF CHOICE

*L*ots of brochures come in the mail, and I like to look through them. I call it my fun mail: business brochures, medical brochures, and gadget catalogs. One particular brochure came about a week ago, and it said, "Here's a sure cure for high blood pressure." It was advice that this writer's grandmother had given him some years before. The advice was simply, "Let it."

For instance, if it threatens rain, let it. That's the cure for high blood pressure.

In this same letter was another little blurb, the story of an art critic who was nearly ninety years old. This art critic said he would gladly beg on a street corner for all the spare minutes that passersby could give him, because life was so precious to him.

This is the basis for the talk this evening, "The Right of Choice." So many people today fall into the myth of the victim consciousness—as if someone else could ever be responsible for the trouble that comes to them. Yet, from the ECK teachings, we know of reincarnation and karma. This perspective lets us look at our follies from a broader scope than most of our neighbors.

So many people today fall into the myth of the victim consciousness—as if someone else could ever be responsible for the trouble that comes to them.

Usually people think their failure in life is a social problem of some kind. They didn't grow up in the right part of the world or the right society; they had so many hardships. In other words, they failed because they were in the wrong place at the wrong time.

In ECK we realize we are in the right place at the right time, no matter what our circumstances may be.

We have put ourselves where we are today. I feel this is the single most important distinction between the ECK teachings and many of the other religious teachings that are in the world today. Of course, there are other paths that teach karma and reincarnation. Millions of people hold these beliefs. But millions of people do not hold the belief and the knowledge that we are Soul and we move to the Light and Sound of God—the Light and Sound of God being divine love.

In ECK we realize we are in the right place at the right time, no matter what our circumstances may be.

DARSHAN

I asked that the lights in the hall be turned up again this evening. I know it's not the usual setting in an auditorium where someone's speaking onstage. You dim the lights so if anyone in the audience wants to, they can sleep without being spotted.

But someone explained to the people in charge of the lights, "This is the time of the Darshan."

I like to see you. It's a very important time. Spiritually this won't mean anything to someone outside of ECK. But in ECK, we know that there can be a very important inner connection, Soul to Soul. And this connection can occur during the Darshan.

Some of you have traveled many thousands of miles, literally from the other side of the earth, to be here. And your journey is as important—and no less important—than someone's who came to the seminar from Atlanta. Soul is Soul, and Soul has this desire to go home to God.

This is the quest for happiness that people misunderstand today. They want to be happy, and so they take the path of pleasure. But it is all necessary for the total experience of Soul. Because at the end of the line, with complete experience, each of you will then become a Co-worker with God.

WHAT IS A CO-WORKER WITH GOD?

Becoming a Co-worker with God is hard to explain. People say, "That sounds like a lot of fun. Really, I'd like to do that sometime." And that's it.

Not everyone will understand this, but if you love your work, your profession, or whatever you're doing, then you'll have some idea what it means to be a Co-worker with God. It simply means that you're doing what you want to do, what you enjoy doing.

You do what gives you the chance for the most spiritual growth and personal fulfillment. That is what it is like to be a Co-worker with God.

To become a Co-worker with God is your goal. And if you enjoy your work, or if you've ever had a job that you've enjoyed, try to go back and imagine the best parts of that. That's a little of what it's like to be a Co-worker with God. A lot of things to do. And in giving, you receive. This is the whole point I try to make in these talks.

YEAR OF THANKSGIVING

This is a Year of Thanksgiving. Before I came out here, my wife mentioned in her gentle way that it

If you love your work, your profession, or whatever you're doing, then you'll have some idea what it means to be a Co-worker with God.

would be good to explain Thanksgiving for what?

I said, "Well, I thought I covered that last night. Thanksgiving for the gift of life."

She said, "You did cover it, but not quite so concisely." So I'm saying it now: if you're wondering what this Year of Thanksgiving is, it's a state of consciousness. And it will go on longer than from one spiritual new year to the next spiritual new year. Thanksgiving is one of the attributes or qualities that come to the person who loves God. To serve others is to love others, and to love others is to serve others.

Sometimes I think back to some of the initiates who were in ECK years ago. I never quite figured out why they ever came to Eckankar. When I began mentioning Soul's goal of spiritual freedom and that the step beyond that was being a Co-worker with God, they said they were so tired of hearing the word *service*. They said they would have a fit if I said it one more time.

I said, "Boy, that's really tough because as long as I'm here, that's what I'm going to be talking about." It's no surprise that some of those people are no longer members of Eckankar.

"I LOVE MY LIFE!"

One of the ECK initiates was helping with the youth program at an ECK seminar. He was putting up some pictures that the children had drawn, hanging them on the wall. Then he'd sit down at a table and prepare other pictures to hang up.

Across from him was this young boy. He was maybe five or six, at the age when kids pretty much speak as they think.

The little guy just looked around, then said to no one in particular, "I love my life! I love my life!" He

> To serve others is to love others, and to love others is to serve others.

was just as pleased with himself as he could be. He didn't care if anybody heard him, he didn't look around to see if anybody was paying attention. He kept talking along this vein, just kept working at what he was doing. Then he said, "All those who love their life, raise their hand." Some of the other little kids were listening, and they raised their hands.

He went on, "I am the oldest man on earth." He didn't care what others said or thought. He was expressing himself as Soul, because Soul has no age. And he was speaking from a purely spiritual viewpoint. He certainly uplifted the spirits of this volunteer who had come into the youth room to help out.

Soul has no age.

And this gentleman said, "This young boy, he wasn't trying to convince anyone of anything. He was just being himself, a joyful, happy Soul, intruding into no one's space, but just declaring his state of happiness." And that was all it took; it rubbed off on everyone in the whole room.

This is also how you are, as members of ECK, when you go out into the world. You don't necessarily sit at a table and say, "I love my life!" But it shows in the things you do, in the love and attention that you give to your work and to the people around you.

They can tell there's something special about you. It doesn't mean you always have a good day—you may have a good day 10 percent of the time. Life is hard. This place wasn't meant to be paradise.

EARTH'S SCHOOLROOM

I looked at the news reports today, and people are again looking for peace on earth. We're seeing reports of "peace breaking out all over."

It almost strikes me as funny. It shows that people do not understand the reason God created this place.

Earth is a schoolroom for Soul. Soul must learn all the spiritual lessons that are necessary before It can become a Co-worker with God. It must learn all the spiritual lessons of life before It can gain spiritual freedom.

When people say, "peace in the Mideast" or "peace in the former Yugoslavia," I just say, "There will be peace when they can settle the land issue." This is just the practical viewpoint; I'm not even getting into the spiritual topic of why there will be no lasting peace on this earth. That's not what is meant to be. This is not the divine plan.

Don't misunderstand me, it doesn't mean that we do not work for peace. Sometimes earth can be a very dreary and desolate place. Our job is to put bright little flowers around so as to lift the spirits of others. You are to be lights—lights of God because you are Soul—to carry happiness and joy into the dark corners of this earth world.

Even though there will never be world peace, you act as if there will be. You work toward it. You work for harmony. You try to make things work out in the workplace and do whatever you can to bring harmony.

Sometimes when I say, "There will never be peace on earth," people who do not understand the ECK teachings say I'm against peace. I'm not against peace. I'm for peace in the heart of each human being. And if there is peace there, it will break out all over. And then there will be peace. But I'm afraid it will have to be in the spiritual worlds.

THE RIGHT OF CHOICE

The right of choice: It's our attitude—the way we look at things—that often determines whether we

Earth is a schoolroom for Soul. It must learn all the spiritual lessons of life before It can gain spiritual freedom.

are happy or miserable, whether we are full of love or full of fear.

An ECK initiate wrote me that her faucet broke. She called her two usual plumbers. But plumber number one was not available. And plumber number two was not available either. So she had to call an economy plumber.

The guy comes out. He used to be from New York and seemed very pleasant. He happened to notice the ECK books on her bookshelf. So as he's working at the sink putting in the new faucet, he starts asking about the ECK teachings. He seemed to be sincere. Otherwise, she wouldn't have been talking to him about the things that were very important and dear to her. After about five minutes, he became very upset and abrasive.

He felt that since her way of salvation was not his own, she was wrong and was therefore fit to take a scolding from him. This upset her, of course. It made her very angry that she would have to defend her religious faith in her own home. So she told him in no uncertain terms, "Go. We're done. You fixed the faucet. Go."

The days went by and after some time, she realized that when she tried to use the dishwasher, it didn't work. Somehow, the dishwasher was no longer connected. So she had to call the plumber again.

She dreaded it because she was afraid of another confrontation—the plumber coming into her home, telling her how she should believe, and in other words, saying that if she didn't believe this way, she would be damned. She thought, *Well, let him be damned. I won't call him.* But again she couldn't get hold of either of the other two plumbers. So she called the economy plumber, and he came. And again he went

It's our attitude—the way we look at things—that often determines whether we are happy or miserable, whether we are full of love or full of fear.

into his little tirade about her religious beliefs. But he got the dishwasher to work, and he left.

Some months later, just within the period of warranty—I know it sounds a little hard to believe— she noticed that the new leakless faucet was leaking.

At this point, she had a choice. She could either call plumber one or two, who this time would gladly come out, but she would have to pay the entire bill. Or she could call the economy plumber, and he'd just do it for free to make his work right. So she called the economy plumber. He was to arrive that afternoon.

> *If only she could fill herself with love when problems like this came up, she knew she'd probably coast right through them.*

That morning she began writing a letter to me. Her heart was full of love, and she realized that she was having such a hard time with this plumber only because of her fear. If only she could fill herself with love when problems like this came up, she knew she'd probably coast right through them. As she wrote her letter, the phone rang. It was the economy plumber. Was it possible, he wondered, to come over and fix the faucet now instead of in the afternoon as planned? She said, "OK, come on over."

A few minutes later, he arrived; he knew what the problem was and got to work. They didn't have to talk about it. He went to the kitchen, and she continued to write her letter to me. And as she wrote, she was filled with love.

When the man finished, she just said, "Goodbye." This time, he was in a hurry to get somewhere, and there was no confrontation.

She realized how important it was for her to write that particular letter to me at that time. In other words, it was a matter of choice. She could have put down her pen and become very anxious and angry as she had been in the preceding months, where she would start mental arguments with this man: "Who are you to tell me what to believe?" "What makes you so special?" All these things kept going around and around and around in her mind. The more they spun around, the angrier she would become. But on this particular day, she realized that if she were ever going to break the cycle that was hurting her, there was no better time than now. It was her choice. And the encounter went very nicely.

CHANGE IN CONSCIOUSNESS

We also have a choice when something new and strange comes into our neighborhood, like new neighbors. Another member of ECK, a Canadian, was mentioning that there had been an old house next to his father's place. Some people came and demolished the house. And not long after, a mansion rose right next door.

The son would go over to mow his father's lawn because he could do it in just an hour whereas it would take his father all day. The house was demolished right around the time he got his inner Second Initiation. New neighbors moved in when he got his Second Initiation on the outer.

The Second Initiation generally occurs after two years of study in ECK. I want to be very sure that anyone who comes to the teachings of ECK is comfortable with them. And at this time, the individual is invited to take an initiation in the Sound and Light of God. It's a short ceremony. It takes anywhere from half an hour to an hour. The initiate receives a personal word which fine-tunes you to the life stream of God, Divine Spirit.

Divine Spirit is not a person. "A force" is not even the correct way to speak of It. The best we can usually

Divine Spirit is not a person. "A force" is not even the correct way to speak of It.

do is to say It's the Light and Sound of God, the Voice of God, the creative force that made all creation. The Word. And the Word went forth. In the beginning was the Word. This sort of thing. This is Divine Spirit going forth to create.

WORKING OFF KARMA

This is what the individual Soul connects with at the Second Initiation. His or her karma is taken over by the Mahanta, the Living ECK Master and given back to the individual to work off in an orderly, forward-moving manner.

We're not saying the teachings of ECK are a panacea for all ills. They are not. You are facing yourself.

Sometimes the karma works off in the dream state or in some other way. For instance, people have car accidents in the dream state instead of having to go through them out here. There are other cases where people have the accident out here, but they are miraculously saved from very severe problems. But we're not saying the teachings of ECK are a panacea for all ills. They are not. You are facing yourself. Sometimes there are more serious things that we must face—not only to pay off a past debt, but also to grow spiritually.

These debts are never fed to the individual out of malice or spite, saying, "You did a bad thing and now you must pay." The Lords of Karma do that; that is under another system. When Soul enters the path of ECK, the Lords of Karma stand to the side, and the spiritual affairs of the individual Soul come under the Mahanta. You can shortcut many of the problems. And the way you shortcut them is through the Spiritual Exercises of ECK.

You make a conscious effort to align yourself or put yourself in tune with Divine Spirit. And you do that by chanting a spiritual word, such as HU.

LAWN CARE

This ECK initiate had just had his inner and outer Second Initiation, which outwardly showed up as the destruction of an old house and the building of a new mansion. And so, being used to caring for his father's lawn, he knew things about grass. He thought people were just born knowing that. As he said, "You're born with knowing when to cut the grass, when to water it in good weather, when to water in a drought, and when to weed."

The family that moved in next door came from Hong Kong. The people had lived in high-rise apartments. When they moved in, they had sod put down for their new lawn, but they didn't know how to take care of it.

The family believed that grass would grow by itself. That the only reason you water it is to make it grow faster, which then means you've got to cut it. That seemed an awful waste of energy. Being very efficient with their time, they didn't realize you had to water the grass just to keep it alive. So before they figured it out, some of the sod had turned yellow and was on the verge of dying.

When the son came over to cut his father's grass, he didn't want to tell the new family how to take care of their lawn. He waited until they asked questions. They came up and watched him. While they were talking he mentioned, "You really ought to water this grass, once a week when it's regular weather, and less for cloudy or rainy periods."

Pretty soon the family wanted him to give them a whole schedule of when to water, when to fertilize, when to weed, and when to mow.

"I couldn't do that," he told them. "Sometimes it's a drought, sometimes it's rainy." The family didn't realize that you had to change according to the weather. But the ECKist helped them as much as he could.

One day, when he was at his father's house cutting the grass, he saw why they hated cutting the grass. The lawnmower they had needed a catcher in back, but they didn't want to put the bag on. It made it very heavy to push this mower around. So they took the bag off. And whoever was pushing the mower got grass thrown in his face.

The ECKist knew it was a dangerous way to operate the mower, because any little stone or twig on the lawn could come flying back. Without that protective bag to catch it, a flying stone could cause injuries. So as soon as they gave him an opening, he explained that to them.

He said, "Use the bag on there. It's also a safety feature."

The heart of this man began to open and expand because he chose to be available to help.

It impressed him that the members of this family were so open. They never showed any embarrassment about not knowing everything there was to know about grass.

As this went along, the heart of this man began to open and expand, too, because he chose to be available to help them if they asked. Maybe they know things that I don't know, he realized, things that are very necessary in life.

One of the things might be, How could they afford that mansion? He wasn't thinking like this, though, but the people obviously knew something he didn't.

Because of the political situation in Hong Kong — in 1997, it will revert to China — some of the people there are moving to Canada and other countries, leaving early. He understood that.

A BOX OF DONUTS

One night, the ECKist was holding an ECK introductory class and there were other ECKists there. After the event was over, they generally went to a donut shop. But that particular night, he didn't feel like going to the donut shop. He went over to his father's place instead.

To his surprise there was a whole box of donuts there. His father explained that the neighbors had brought it over. Since the neighbors from Hong Kong didn't know what kind of donuts they liked, they had bought all different kinds just to make sure that somewhere in there was a donut that the father and son would like.

The ECKist realized there was a balance between these two families. The people from Hong Kong were probably lonesome. They had left all their family and friends behind. They were in a strange land. And worse, they had a lawn.

And on the Canadian side of the equation there was the old house that used to stand there, and of course people who used to live there had old feelings and thoughts. Then to have people move in who were from a totally different culture, the neighbors found it hard to say, "OK, we accept you with open hearts." They might say, "Well, I'm not so sure I want to do that because our differences are too great."

The ECKist didn't let that bother him. He opened his heart to the family from Hong Kong, and they, in turn, opened their hearts to him and his father.

GIVING OTHERS FREEDOM

Again, it was a matter of choice. The ECKist recognized his father's new neighbors as spiritual beings, as Soul, and as such, he gave them the freedom to either accept his help or reject it. He didn't push his knowledge of lawn care on them.

Whether it's knowledge of lawn care or knowledge of spiritual laws or spiritual beliefs or anything else, we don't have a right to push our beliefs upon anyone else. Nor does anyone else have the right to push their beliefs on us. This is part of the freedom of Soul.

God made so many religions so there would be one for every person who wanted one. And every person and every group of people has uniquely different beliefs.

I often think of some of the different groups of Lutherans. An outsider looks at them and says, "Their differences in belief are so slight, it makes one wonder why they aren't all just one big group." But that's how it is. There are many, many different levels of consciousness in a society, in the world. And the divine order has provided a way for each group or each individual to rise to their own level. And this is the reason for the different religions on earth.

Why should any one religion try to suppress another simply because they feel it's their right to do so? This is a violation of spiritual law. You cannot force others to do your will and call it God's will.

GOLDEN BUTTERFLY

We also have the right of choice when it comes to arranging our daily life.

Sometimes we don't understand that the tragedy we face has all kinds of experiences involved—if we handle it a certain way, we will end a chain of karma that has probably been going on for centuries. We will resolve a debt that needs to be repaid before one of the

God made so many religions so there would be one for every person who wanted one.

You cannot force others to do your will and call it God's will.

individuals involved can gain spiritual freedom.

A man in Africa was very saddened one day when his young daughter died suddenly. The mother had taken the child to the hospital, but it hadn't been for any great illness. Suddenly, because a wrong inoculation was administered by the head nurse, his daughter had passed over to the other side.

As a father, he was very distraught, and he asked the owner of the hospital and the head nurse to come and explain why his daughter was gone. What had they done?

"We didn't do anything," they said. "It was just a certain medicine that didn't work."

But the man wasn't satisfied with that. He was so distraught when the nurse told him of his daughter's death that he just wanted to hit her in anger and frustration.

The day of the funeral arrived. All the neighbors in the community came. The link between families is very strong in some of these communities, and the community came to help him bury his dead child.

But as they stood by the grave, they saw a beautiful golden butterfly hovering over the crowd. Then it flew away. As the father looked closer at the dirt around the grave, he saw a caterpillar. He realized that Soul going into a higher state is like the caterpillar transforming into a butterfly.

While this was going on, he also saw white-and-blue birds — about a dozen of them — flying in a circle right above the crowd.

Yet through all this, he was very upset. He went home, wrapped himself in a sheet, and began to cry and cry. And he said, "Mahanta, why have you allowed my daughter to leave like this?"

Soon he fell asleep. And while he was asleep, the

Mahanta came to him and said, "Have you learned nothing from the ECK teachings? Have you learned nothing? My son, I have tried to teach you, and yet you carry on like a child."

Suddenly, the scene changed and a room appeared. There was his daughter. She came running up to him and hugged him. After he had hugged her a little while, she began squirming and wanted to get down and run off and play.

The Mahanta said to the father, "Just wait a minute. I want to show you something. Please hold your daughter."

A TV appeared on the wall. A movie began to play. And the Master said, "We are now going back to the Oracle at Delphi." As they watched, a scene appeared. Five warriors were in mortal combat. Two of the warriors were the parents of this girl, and this little girl was also fighting. In the scene she was a very strong man. The warrior had taken the life of two other warriors. But then the two warriors who were the husband and wife finally overcame this warrior who was very strong.

The Mahanta explained, "In that lifetime, your daughter was the very strong warrior and killed these other two warriors in battle. One of the warriors is the owner of the hospital. The other is the head nurse. If you had struck the head nurse in the hospital, she would have died and this would have extended the karma for another round."

"The only way this karma could resolve," the Mahanta told him, "was for your young daughter to pay it back here, so she could be released from her last life on this earth."

Then the father realized that this collection of characters—himself, his wife, his daughter, the owner of the hospital, and the head nurse—weren't just casual strangers. They had been together before, and they had hurt each other. In this experience, the entire karmic chain was broken. It allowed the daughter to move forward spiritually and never have to return to this earth.

His daughter was now so full of light and happiness. The Master said, "This is how you knew her, and that's why she has appeared to you in this form." The daughter could now go on to higher, happier places.

Once he saw and understood this, the man woke up and told his grieving wife the story. They could still grieve the absence of their child, but now they could also understand why this apparent injustice had to occur to their daughter. The man realized it wasn't injustice at all, but perfect justice.

ON A MOUNTAIN ROAD

Other times, the matter of choice is not so clear, and the individual works with it a long time, trying to understand.

A businessman was driving through the mountains. He was coming home from a business trip, and he got into an accident. When it was over, he realized he had been saved from serious injury, but at the same time, he had gone through this accident. He was trying to resolve what was involved.

It was a moonlit night in January, in the northeastern part of the country. It had been a very pleasant day. The temperature was warm for that time of year—about fifty degrees. As he drove, he saw beautiful moonlight coming through the trees.

He figured that the temperature had dropped about five degrees in the last little while, but as he

In this experience, the entire karmic chain was broken.

came over a hill, he saw an accident ahead. He started to slow his car down, but he realized his brakes weren't working at all. He was on a sheet of ice. He didn't know what to do.

Next to him was the guardrail, then a drop-off, and a river far below.

He took his foot off the brake pedal and tried to steer around the two cars. For a minute, he thought he was going to make it. But one of the cars was right in his way. So he hit the brakes. His car went into a spin, and he figured this was his time to leave. He shut his eyes, sang HU, and put his attention on the Mahanta.

There was an explosion of sound as his car hit the guardrail, and then silence.

During that silence, his car had jumped forty feet, down the side of the mountain, plowed through a couple of trees, and finally came to rest against a large tree 120 feet farther down the mountainside.

The man sat there for three to five minutes. He thought he was dead. It had been such a terrible accident. He'd gone over the cliff, down the side of the mountain. He sat there waiting for the Mahanta to come and get him. Finally, he opened his eyes. He looked around and saw his car. It was just a mess.

He crawled out of the broken rear window and looked way up at the guardrail. Someone was looking down—all the way down—at him in the darkness. But before he could wave, the person disappeared.

So he made his way, very slowly, up the side of this steep mountain, and finally he came to the road. There were some police cars at the scene of the accident. As the man came walking out of the darkness, he startled the police officers. They didn't know anybody else was around. This was in a deserted area. "Where'd you come from?" they asked him.

He said, "From down there. Didn't somebody look over the edge of the guardrail?"

They said, "No. We were looking at this accident."

And he said, "There's another one down there."

The officers looked over the edge of the cliff, and one of the officers came back, looking very seriously at the man. "Only God saved you," he said.

His car had hit the last tree, and that tree had held the weight. The officer said if that tree had broken and the car crashed through, it would have been another two hundred feet straight down into an icy river.

The ECKist was wondering, "What was this all about?"

An Experience That Changes Your Life

An experience like this will change your life. First of all, it will turn you into a seeker—in the sense of looking for the answer to why you had protection in such a startling way. Why did you have the Master's protection? Why were you spared?

A person's life will take a turn from that point on. Things that used to mean a lot won't mean quite as much anymore.

Generally an experience like that tends to open the heart. Divine Spirit was simply saying, "It's time to wake up. There's more to life than what you've been doing. There's more to life. Keep doing what you're doing, but look at it with the spiritual eyes. Look with the spiritual eyes."

The officer later explained what had happened. The temperature had dropped fifteen degrees in twenty minutes. The falling temperatures had caused

Divine Spirit was simply saying, "It's time to wake up. There's more to life than what you've been doing."

black ice to form on the roadway. This driver had never heard of black ice before.

If any of you have ever hit black ice while you were driving, you know. The road can look perfectly clear. Suddenly, you hit black ice and there you go. (I've had most of these experiences. You don't want them.) So whenever you see a very sharp drop in temperature—usually right around evening or when a cold front comes in—be very careful because black ice doesn't show.

Earning the Right

A woman was very ill. She was running a fever. The illness had been going on for weeks. It's just the flu," she told herself. She thought she'd get over it. But she just got sicker and sicker. Finally, she went to the hospital and had an exam.

The doctor said, "Looks like there's an infected mass in one of your Fallopian tubes." The treatment for this was to go into the hospital and have intravenous antibiotics for five days or so. So she was in the hospital, hooked up to all the tubes, having this medicine going into her. But on the third night, when she went to sleep, the Inner Master, the Mahanta, showed up.

On the third night, when she went to sleep, the Inner Master, the Mahanta, showed up.

"Come along," he said. "We're going to see something."

And she said, "What for?"

He said, "We want to see how your body's doing."

A scene opened up in a Roman coliseum. Gladiators were fighting with great, clanging swords. It was dusty, bloody, and dirty. The iron swords made a terrible clashing sound as they struck each other.

When the woman came out of the experience, she knew that her body was going through an enormous battle.

On the evening of the fourth day, her doctor said, "Your fever's not down. I can't let you go home if your fever's this high. We'll just have to keep you a little longer."

Not long after, she found herself in a higher state of consciousness again, in the Soul body. This was Soul Travel. Her body was very sick in the hospital, but as Soul, she found herself at a meeting with the ECK Masters. They were discussing her fate.

The ECK Masters asked her, "What is your goal in life?" And she said, "To serve God."

They said to her, "Your body's very sick. And we're looking at what your spiritual duties can be in the other worlds."

She said, "OK," and they began discussing it around the table.

Then one of the ECK Masters asked her, "What is your goal in life?"

And she said, "To serve God."

"Well, you're ready to drop this body. You can go on into the other planes."

She said, "I have a daughter who is still in her early twenties. I would have a hard time watching the grief of my daughter because she wouldn't understand why I didn't come through this. So for that reason, I would like to go back."

The ECK Master said to her, "All right. You have earned the right of choice."

This woman had developed herself spiritually through the teachings of ECK. She had put herself in tune with Divine Spirit, with the Light and Sound of God, so that at this point she was becoming a Co-worker with the Mahanta, and then later a Co-worker with God. She had earned the right of choice.

AWAKENING THE
GOD-KNOWLEDGE WITHIN

Being in ECK involves self-responsibility. No one cares if you do the spiritual exercises or if you don't.

Being in ECK involves self-responsibility.

But if you care about yourself, you should care whether you do them. Because you have this spiritual tool to rise in consciousness so that instead of being a victim of life—as so many people wrongly believe they are—you will have choices.

The choices don't just happen. You make them. If you make a series of right choices, they will spiritualize you. In ECK, this upliftment comes through the Spiritual Exercises of ECK. This is all I have to offer you.

My talks go several different ways, and so do the writings. Some of them are instructive where I give actual rules: Do this or that if you want to accomplish this or that. But many of the talks are purely for inspiration. Because as Soul, you have the God-knowledge within you. My main job is to awaken the knowledge and love for the divine things that are already in your heart. You are Soul. You are a child of God.

And your spiritual destiny is to become a Co-worker with God, to spread divine love to all those around you.

*ECK Worldwide Seminar, Atlanta, Georgia,
Saturday, October 22, 1994*

The dream took place in a room that was beyond the definition of time or space. In a big book, the woman found a word, *Wah Z.*

3

A LARGER ROOM

---

he title of the talk this morning is "A Larger Room."

This summer I missed the first seminar in thirteen years—the ECK European Seminar. I waited until the very last minute to decide that it would be better not to go.

Around last October my health began to go downhill. I'd noticed at the Worldwide and Springtime Seminars that walking from the front door to the gate in airport terminals had become a long, long distance.

WHEN THE CYCLE CHANGES

For a long time it was difficult to figure out what was going on. After an auto accident in 1991, I had problems healing. I wasn't healing right. Even now, some things are still healing.

I stopped rather suddenly when my brakes failed in 1991. They failed in two ways: first of all, the back brakes were completely out of adjustment. And there was an air bubble in the brake line besides. So at one point, I had no brakes at all. It happened in city traffic instead of on the freeway, which was good. But

It was almost ten years since I had become the Mahanta, the Living ECK Master, and there were all kinds of things trying to prevent me from making it an even ten.

I was still going along city-traffic speed, which was thirty miles an hour, and came to a very sudden stop.

It was almost ten years since I had become the Mahanta, the Living ECK Master, 1981 to 1991, and there were all kinds of things trying to prevent me from making it an even ten. I was starting the next cycle.

I got through that period, but the healing didn't come along very well. I kept going for chiropractic treatments and did other things. But after 1991, I stopped driving. I just said, "The risk isn't worth it to Eckankar." Also, for many months, I wasn't in much shape to do any driving. I had to lie on ice packs from twenty minutes to an hour several times a day. So I preserved myself very well during that time.

HOME SICKNESS

For several years, I would come home from a seminar tired but strong. Then last October, I began to notice that when we had been home for a few hours, I would begin to get sick. But then after an hour or two more, my wife and I would put our attention on the ECK work which we had to do and forget about how we felt.

I couldn't figure out what was wrong. I haven't put much attention on my health since I came into this position in 1981. I just took care of myself as best I could.

Then I began to get very sick last October. From October through April I had fever and chills constantly, as if I had malaria from one of my trips overseas. When I got real cold, the only way I could get warm was to lie down and rest.

Soon I was resting one, two, or three times a day, from half an hour to an hour. I was going downhill.

A LARGER ROOM

I'm not speaking of this as a unique experience, because we all have our good days and we have our bad days. We have youth, then we have middle age, and we deal with it the best we can.

And as we go into middle age, we enter a larger room with new experiences. As we go from middle age to advanced age, we find we go to still another room. And each room should always be larger—where we have new experiences. We have to deal with things that used to be easy and suddenly we find they're not.

As we go into middle age, we enter a larger room with new experiences. Each room should always be larger—where we have new experiences.

A CLEAN BILL OF HEALTH

Finally, I told my wife, "OK, I've got to do something about my health." I was very sick. There were many, many symptoms: heart palpitations, fever, chills, and pressure in the head. All these, and a lot more besides. And I was getting weaker and weaker, spending most of my time in bed except for the time I was doing the ECK work. I had to regulate my time very carefully so that I could get everything done. And I continued writing, even as I do now.

I went to a doctor. He was a good man. He did over fifty-two tests, and they all came back negative. He said, "I have to give you a clean bill of health."

And I was barely able to stand. I was wondering, "What is going on here?"

But I put my attention on it, and I knew that the ECK would bring these things to my attention. It would bring one thing after another, and then I would just absorb the different things that I needed to know and deal with it. So just to be sure, I went to another doctor and had another set of exams. He too finally said, "I have to give you a clean bill of health." And

I was sicker than ever.

This always strikes me as funny. To the medical profession, medicine cannot fail. If I'm sick and they don't know why, they think it's in my head. So when they come to the end of the road, they ask, "Well, would you like to see the staff psychologist?"

I said, "No, thank you. I've been there."

There's a good rule I read somewhere: If you go to a doctor and the meetings begin to eat away at your self-esteem, don't go anymore.

If you go to a doctor and the meetings begin to eat away at your self-esteem, don't go anymore.

A NEW HOME

Now I was finding out what was the matter. We had lived in our home for six years. There was this nice swamp in back with all kinds of spores. I fed the little animals, and they would fertilize the lawn. There was also a major freeway a block away.

And there were high-voltage wires right beside our home. Both offices and our bedroom were on the side of the house by the wires. Downstairs was our family room and our exercise room; we spent all our time on that side of the house.

Right about this time, the ECK sold the house out from under us. We had been renting, and the owners now decided the real-estate market was reviving and it was time to unload the place quickly. So they sold it. That meant that within a month's time, we had to find a new place. And of course my wife and I are thinking, *How are we going to keep up the ECK work that we're doing and all the schedules* —because everything's on a schedule—*and have time to move?*

We usually don't have ECKists come to our home, but for the first time, we had some ECKists visit. The gentleman had had sensitivities to electromagnetic radiation years ago, and also to molds and spores.

He walked into our home and within just a very few minutes, he became very ill. He said he wouldn't have lasted more than a couple of days in the house, and we had been here all this time.

ELECTROMAGNETIC RADIATION

In my files, I had information about electromagnetic radiation. I'll just call them EMRs for short. EMR is produced by things like microwave ovens, fluorescent lights, cars, and planes.

None of this had ever bothered me before, and it doesn't bother most people. Hair dryers, ovens, and bedside clocks — they have very high levels of electromagnetic radiation. I found that even the little black box on our answering machine produces a high level of electromagnetic radiation. I was surrounded by it. So I got a little meter that tells how much EMR there is in a room. I checked our home and found there were hot spots and cool spots.

I was finding out that I was sensitive to these things, and I had to try to reverse the process. These EMRs play havoc with the electrical impulses in the body; they can burn the nervous system. It's like a sunburn. When you get a very bad sunburn, for a long time you don't want to be anywhere near the sun, because even the smallest exposure is very painful.

EMRs were interfering with the electrical impulses to my heart and to my lungs.

I found that these EMRs were interfering with the electrical impulses to my heart and to my lungs. And I could eat fewer and fewer foods.

So, with the help of some friends, we moved to another place. It was away from the high-voltage wires and the transformer we had outside our home. On the day of the move, I did nothing. I had no more energy, no more strength. I was about at the very, very bottom. As low as I've ever been.

GAINING STRENGTH

Since then, I have found ways to balance my diet. I had been doing things with diet before; I'd been very careful. Now I've gone on a low-fat diet, Dean Ornish's diet for reversing heart disease. I did it on my own because I wasn't getting help from the doctors. They said my cholesterol level was good "for my age."

I did some other things. I got devices to help neutralize the scrambled photons that occur when the electromagnetic radiation is strong.

And in the process, I've learned that there are a lot of other people in much worse shape than I was, doing the best they could with one kind of environmental illness or another. And some of these illnesses just boggle the mind.

Every day I put myself into the hands of the ECK as I always do, and whatever Its will is, so be it.

I'm doing everything I can to meet my commitments here at the seminar. Every day I put myself into the hands of the ECK as I always do, and whatever Its will is, so be it. And this is just how it is.

I have been gaining strength. But I canceled my trip to the 1995 ECK South Pacific Seminar in Australia which will occur this January because the long plane trip would be extremely hard. And so for a year or so, I'm going to put my attention very strongly on healing. And it's coming about.

After I couldn't make it to Europe, I spoke with my daughter, who had just turned twenty-one. We were talking on the phone, and she said, "Hey Dad, I heard you took a vacation." She was referring to not going to the ECK seminar in Europe. I just said, "Right. I took a vacation." I didn't say any more.

My vacations are coming to the ECK seminars and being with you. To me, this is my vacation.

Twelve-Year Cycles

This morning, I was meeting with some ECK initiates. "Well, what happens?" they asked me. "A lot of us are going into the twelve-year cycle of when we came in ECK, too, when we took the Second Initiation."

I said, "Don't worry about it," because it's different for everyone.

Twelve-year cycles can begin anytime. They can begin at birth, and then we have cycles ending and beginning at twelve, twenty-four, thirty-six, forty-eight, sixty years old, and so on. At each one of these twelve-year cycles—which keys entirely to the physical and social development—we find there are good turning points. Interesting turning points.

Each one of these turning points is about entering a larger room. For the twelve-year-old, it's leaving childhood and going into the first stages of adulthood.

In our society, we don't think of twelve-year-olds as adults. And they aren't. They're just beginning to learn, they're just on the threshold of adulthood. This threshold lasts until the second cycle, at age twenty-four. By that time, you are pretty much a weathered young adult. Life has tossed you about in its storms enough so that you have some idea that you are not superhuman. You've learned a little bit about the frailties of the human condition. You realize that there are things that you need to polish up before you can become a greater spiritual being.

Life has tossed you about in its storms enough so that you have some idea that you are not superhuman.

What Can Life Teach Me Today?

The title "A Larger Room" fits this talk because as you go through life—especially for those of you who are in ECK—each morning should be a revelation. Each morning you should be awaking in a larger room, in a larger state of spiritual consciousness where you say, "Well, I wonder what life has to teach me today."

Then go forth with love as much as you can and meet life on your own terms.

Because, after all, your life and all life in general basically depends upon how you look at it. Some people have all kinds of good things brought to them, and they have no appreciation for them because it all came to them too easily. Other people who have the good things of life have worked hard for them and appreciate them sincerely, with their whole heart.

And it's the same with other things in life. Life is like the weather. There are times of flood, and there are times of drought. And we like the seasons in between where there is enough rain but not too much; a little sun, but not too much. But life has its droughts and floods.

The question then is What state of consciousness faces these? Where are you at? What are you looking for? What are you expecting from life?

SOUND OF TRAINS

Last night after my talk, my wife asked, "Did you hear the train when it went past?" I said, "No, I guess my mouth was open. When my mouth is open, my ears are shut."

If you're at all interested in country music, at least the old songs, they always had a lot of train songs. Train songs where somebody's in prison, and they say, "If I had it my way, I'd move the train a little farther away because every time I hear it, I get this longing for freedom."

Sometimes, the ECK just sets up the sound of a train whistle. It's saying, "Time to travel spiritually, and with the desire to have spiritual freedom, to go other places and eventually home to God."

A Different Direction

To go back to the illness again, I noticed that one of the things that throws off a fair amount of electromagnetic radiation was my little computer. So I've been writing all the discourses and all the articles by hand with no benefit of spell-checker, grammar-checker, or style-checker.

In the years since I've been using these programs on the computer, I learned more about the rules of grammar and of style. I used the computer programs to educate myself. Even if I'm never able to use a computer again, I will at least have these writing skills to use to present the teachings of ECK. In fact, I now find writing by hand to be faster than on the computer. I have to compose practically the entire discourse before I start; it's all done in my head. And then I just write.

Then, very often, I find that the ECK steers me in a different direction. I plan to write in one direction; I've got the outline in my mind. Then suddenly It sends an image through of an entirely different subject. And so I write about that. I write until I have explained and written about that image. Sometimes it's a story, sometimes just an illustration.

One of the most difficult tasks I had back in 1981 was when I began writing for ECK. First, I started writing by hand. I was very slow. There were a lot of crossed-out words. It was a terrible-looking piece of paper. Then I took another step. I used a typewriter. There were a lot of crossovers and strikeouts.

Time to travel spiritually, and with the desire to have spiritual freedom, to go other places and eventually home to God.

Eventually I got on a word processor. This was before there were too many computer programs. Then I got rid of the word processor and got a real computer. Then I learned how to use the grammar-checker. I just worked with it.

HOW TO WRITE BETTER

When you're writing, you learn, you find, or you discover that there's always more to learn. No matter how well you wrote yesterday, when you read it over a few days later, you say, "Oh, I wish I'd done a few things differently." You often wish you'd written it a little cleaner, a little better.

So time went on. I picked up the spell-checker after the grammar-checker because the computer programs were able to do it. I also got a style-checker that showed how to vary the length of sentences and the length of paragraphs. It made me more aware of these aspects of writing.

Now here I am, back at square one, like in 1981 at the beginning of that twelve-year cycle, writing by hand, but writing in a totally different way than I did before.

What are you doing with the tools you have? Are you using them as a crutch? Or are you using them as a teacher?

So I also have come into a larger room. But while I was working with all these computer aids, I didn't let them do the work for me. I was using them as teachers to teach me how to write better and more clearly.

When I hear people complaining that this spell-checker is better than the one they have or that grammar-checker is better than theirs, maybe one is better than the other. But basically, the important question is What are you doing with the tools you have? Are you using them as a crutch? Or are you using them as a teacher? Use all the training aids—

everything that comes into your life—as a teacher. Not as a crutch, not as an excuse.

LESSONS OF LIFE

I think if more people looked at what life has to offer them as teaching aids from Divine Spirit, they would be better spiritual and human beings instead of being victims.

Some say, "So and so did that to me, and that's why I have failed." But there are so many examples of people who have had real hardships—in health or coming from other countries where there were wars, where they lost limbs, where they lost family members. Those people have had hardships. And people who have served in the wars from our own country. They came back. They coped.

It is the people who have had a relatively soft life who are crying, "I'm a victim." And it's because they are spiritual infants. They haven't learned to take the lessons of life as their own lessons, as lessons they have created for themselves. In other words, these people are refusing to walk into a larger room. And it's sad.

Take the lessons of life as teachers and not as crutches. If you can just remember this—the concept of a larger room—it will help you immensely.

Take responsibility for yourself, for your condition in life. No matter how bad a situation is, even at work.

I've been in the position myself all too often where out of the necessity, I had this driving force that said, "I've got to take care of myself." I'm not talking about if you're retired or there's a serious health condition and you now have to accept Social Security or whatever. That is part of living; it is necessary. I'm talking

Take the lessons of life as teachers and not as crutches.

about people who are in good health and strong.

Take responsibility. Recognize that this entire lifetime is a high spiritual experience—or it could be. And whether or not it will be depends upon how you look at it. It depends upon your attitude.

Recognize that this entire lifetime is a high spiritual experience—or it could be.

INITIATIONS ARE LIKE LARGER ROOMS

One of the ECK initiates was planning to go to an ECK seminar. A few weeks before the seminar, he was driving to work one morning, going a little bit too fast, pushing. He had gotten up a little late, and then he had to hurry. So on the way to work, he got into an auto accident.

No one was seriously injured. He went to his doctor immediately after to get treatment. The doctor happened to be an ECKist.

The patient and the doctor, both being ECKists, began to talk about the upcoming seminar. The man asked the doctor, "Are you planning to go to the ECK seminar that's coming up?" The doctor said, "Actually I'm planning to step back from ECK for a while." This ECKist couldn't understand this—the doctor was a Higher Initiate. He said, "Why would a Higher Initiate stand back from ECK?"

The doctor explained, "When I became a Fifth Initiate, I thought I would know everything." And he had been very disappointed. He thought he'd know everything.

This other initiate wasn't a Higher Initiate. He had this incredible understanding. "But," he said, "initiations are like walking into ever-larger rooms where you discover what you don't know." This statement took the doctor aback because he hadn't thought of that.

Plus Element

This is truly what life is all about. Even the ECK Masters find the plus element in life.

We have this mystique about masters, "the perfected ones." They're perfected at a certain level. But in the absolute sense of the word, there is always one more step to go spiritually. And this applies to all the ECK Masters.

For this reason, there are ECK Masters at one level, another level, and another level, and a higher level, and so on. There are ECK Masters with different levels of responsibility. Each one is working at his or her level, wherever they feel spiritually comfortable.

I never claim that I know everything, because to say such a thing is silly. And for people to believe that a Master should know everything is equally silly.

Even the ECK Masters find the plus element in life. There is always one more step to go spiritually.

The Easy Way

A woman became a member of Eckankar and received *The Easy Way Discourses.* And then one night, she had a dream. She found herself with the Mahanta—this is the Inner Master, the inner form of myself. They were with a group of people—strangers but they weren't strangers.

The dream took place in a room that was beyond the definition of time or space. And in this room was a big book, just a single book. The group of people stood around it, and each in turn would flip to one page or another and pick out a word. Each person got a word.

The woman found a word, but she hadn't been in ECK long enough to know what the word meant. The word was *Wah Z.* For some reason, she liked the word. She'd never heard it before. She hadn't come to it in the inner teachings, the more advanced teachings, and she hadn't run across it in any of the outer writings. She didn't realize that Wah Z, or sometimes Z for short, is the name of the Inner Master.

So she convinced all the people in this group on the inner planes to chant this word with her. And so they all chanted Wah Z. She liked the sound of it.

Suddenly a light came into the room, a warm, bright light that reached into the very depths of her heart. It made her feel warm and full of love. As the experience was going on, someone walked into the room where she was sleeping and turned on the bedroom light.

It woke her, and she lost the experience. She was very upset by this, but she tried not to show it.

What she didn't realize is that that person didn't accidentally walk into the room and turn on the light. The ECK—or the Mahanta—arranged for the person to come in just at the highlight of the inner experience. Otherwise the woman would have forgotten her experience.

While she was writing this in her spiritual journal, it suddenly came to her that this was her First Initiation in ECK, as indeed it was. She had entered a larger room. The First Initiation in ECK usually comes during the first year of study of the ECK discourses, when one has made a commitment to the teachings of ECK.

The First Initiation in ECK usually comes during the first year of study of the ECK discourses, when one has made a commitment to the teachings of ECK.

CIRCLE OF LIGHT AND LOVE

A person who hadn't yet made the commitment to become a member of ECK once met an ECKist and said, "Well, I am a member of ECK because I've been reading the books." "Is it the same?" the ECKist asked. They're on different sides of the fence, in a way. One is studying the teachings of ECK from books and the other has made the commitment to become a member of Eckankar and then receive the ECK discourses and other spiritual benefits.

Then the person who was just reading the books noticed that there was an aura of light and love coming from the ECKist. She realized that maybe it does make a difference. Maybe it does make a difference to make a commitment to Divine Spirit because Divine Spirit is the ECK.

So, for those of you who came to this seminar, I think you will find that when you go out those doors today on your way home, you will enter a larger room. This seminar has opened you to a greater capacity for divine love.

Be careful that you don't go out of balance in the first week that you're home. Sometimes when you leave an ECK seminar, there's this feeling of emptiness and loneliness. You say, "I wish I were back at the seminar with others who love God in this particular way." But don't worry. The inner love will come and fill this emptiness in your heart, which is simply more room in your heart.

It takes a little while for divine love to reach in and touch all the corners of your heart.

You've just entered a larger room, and that's often why you feel this emptiness. It takes a little while for divine love to reach in and touch all the corners of your heart.

ECK Worldwide Seminar, Atlanta, Georgia, Sunday, October 23, 1994

Listen to the people around you. Because, after all, if someone's telling you something that is spiritual and positive, this is from the Voice of God.

4

RECOGNIZING GOD'S HELP IN YOUR LIFE

*I*t's a pleasure to be here with you this New Year's Day. I imagine you've all come with your resolutions—to decide how long you'll keep them. From your past track record, I think you have a good idea.

The title of the talk this morning is "Recognizing God's Help in Your Life." I try to talk about this and give stories and examples, because sometimes God's help and love is so commonplace that we don't recognize it until someone points it out. And often, when it comes to demonstrating love, we are kinder and better to other people—especially when we're under stress—than we are to our own loved ones.

We come home after a hard day at the office. We've done it all—we've stretched ourself to the diplomatic end. Now we come home, and we take it out on our mate or our kids. Why? Because we're used to them. They're family.

LEARNING TO LOVE

But I believe Soul's lesson here is to learn how to love God through loving first ourselves and then our family.

Soul's lesson here is to learn how to love God through loving first ourselves and then our family.

I don't know if there's a real cause-and-effect relationship. In other words, do you begin by loving God first, and then you're able to love your family and others in this world? Or do you love others first, and then through loving others, you're then able to love God? I don't know. It may be different for everyone. Maybe it's different at different times.

Often in life, we try to be spiritual. If anyone asks, we say, "We're good people. We lead good lives." But we really don't practice this during the week because we're too busy doing other things that are more important, like staying alive or earning a living—little things like that. We run from place to place with our kids. They've got this or that activity going on. It's a fast pace. Or when we get older, we race from doctor to doctor.

> Often in life, we try to be spiritual. But we really don't practice this during the week because we're too busy.

QUICK STUDY

A friend was telling us about their family dog. The dog is a quick study. At home, a young pup just growing up needs to learn how to behave. She needs to learn that if she sees someone she loves, she doesn't jump on them and drool all over them. Basic discipline. But the puppy wasn't doing very well at home. So the family thought it might be good to take her to one of the training schools for dogs.

So every Wednesday night they take this sweet, loving dog to training school. Of course, they don't have time during the week to work with her, to teach her things like Sit! or Stay! They don't have time for it. So they usually come to class unprepared.

Now this is a very intelligent dog. The other dogs in the class just sit there, looking straight ahead in a dull way or looking around very slowly. But this puppy spends her time studying other dogs and their owners very carefully.

She knows that when you come to dog training class, there is a special way to behave. She doesn't know how it's done because she wasn't taught at home. Her owners didn't have time to work with her at home. So when she comes to the class, she looks around and picks up the behavior as quickly as she can.

And she does very well. At home, when her master says, "Sit!" she won't sit. This is home, you know. Then he says, "Stay!" He backs a couple of steps away. She comes up to him, as if she's saying, "It's home, silly. You don't have to do stuff like that at home." But when she is in discipline class once a week, she'll sit there, looking around the room, watching how other dogs and their masters behave. And then she does the same thing. It's always surprising to the man of the house. In class he says, "Sit!" and she'll actually sit.

Then he'll say, "Stay!" He'll walk a couple of steps away, and she'll stay. And then he'll say, "Come!" And—this is the part she likes—she'll come running up to him.

Life gives us more lessons because we can handle more.

She's a quick study. I guess we're pretty much like that too, as we come to a path that spiritually enlivens us. It means life is putting more and more lessons to us about how to live and gain divine love. And we learn how to give it back to others.

The reason life gives us more lessons is because we can handle more. We've learned the old lessons, the ABCs. Now we can go on to arithmetic and geography and other things.

NEW MATH

When my daughter was studying new math, I had to learn math all over. I found it very interesting.

She was only six or seven years old at the time. And I had never been very good at math in school. But I'd go through it with her.

I'd say, "Look here. This is how this is done, and you can take a shortcut here, right in your head. You can do it like this." She understood, simply because I was explaining it to her. And I was discovering something myself. I've always considered myself to be pretty childlike. If I can learn something, so can anyone else. It worked with my daughter. If I could understand her new math, there was no reason she shouldn't be able to. And of course she could.

It's that way with the lessons from the Holy Spirit, which we call the ECK. It gives us lessons. And if we have the capacity for love—which is all that this life is about—life gives us more experience.

You say, "Maybe I don't want more experience." Because more experience usually means more discomfort of some kind.

The Inner Master always looks out for your spiritual welfare.

It usually means: when I've expected things to go a certain way, all of a sudden my world's turned upside down. The job didn't work out the way I thought. I didn't get the promotion. My health took a turn for the worse, and things like this. So you say, "Maybe I don't want to unfold so fast spiritually if it means having to go through this sort of stuff."

But the Inner Master always looks out for your spiritual welfare.

ADDING SPICE TO LIFE

The Inner Master doesn't look out for the outer side of yourself, the social being that says, "I want things to be pretty and nice like this always. I want the new year to be just like the best of times in the old year."

It doesn't quite work like that. We don't learn and grow if everything is always smooth and pretty and nice. Sometimes you have to get the other experiences in life. It's necessary, like salt and pepper on your food. It adds spice to life.

You don't want to eat a whole meal of black pepper. You want to use a little bit as a seasoning. But when you say, "I don't want too many of life's hard experiences," you mean that you don't want even a little pepper.

But life gives you a little pepper anyway.

We're talking about recognizing God's help in your life. This help is like little presents, believe it or not. But usually we don't think of them as presents.

SURPRISE PACKAGE

The other day, I got a package in the mail. I brought it home, looked at it, and told my wife, "I know the company. It's in St. Paul. But I don't think I've ordered anything from them."

I didn't want to go through the trouble of opening a package of something I didn't order. I don't like packages. It's like life. You say, "What if it doesn't work? What if it doesn't fit?" Especially through mail order. And especially if I'm not sure I've ordered it.

My order file was in another room, so I went to check it.

The package sat there. Anybody else would rip into it. Most of the time, my wife barely gets a package in the door before she rips it open. Sometimes she actually leaves packages until the next morning, though. But I didn't know what to do with this package. So I told her, "I'm not going to rip into that package because then I'll just have to rewrap it. I'd rather just tear a label off and send it back to them if they sent

> *We don't learn and grow if everything is always smooth and pretty and nice.*

somebody else's package to me."

The next morning, my wife said, "Did you check on the package?"

I said, "No. I forgot all about it," and I really had. I'm just not that wild about packages. I usually decide to order something after I've looked at the catalog then put it in my order file for a while. It might stay there for half a year. Then I call to order. "Do you still carry this item?" I ask. If, after all that time, they still do, I'll order it. I like to feel things out before I get something new. Incorporating anything else into my world is a problem, a complexity. And I like things simple. Life is complicated enough without making it more so.

Finally I called the company because I had nothing in my order file. A customer service representative by the name of John answered. "John," I said, "I have this problem." I explained it to him.

John said, "Give me the invoice number."

I said, "But John, it's in the package, and I'm not going to open the package until you can tell me if I ordered it."

John said, "OK." He took my name and checked his computer. After a while he said, "Oh yes, I've got you on the screen here."

"Good," I said. "Did I order this?"

"No, you didn't." Very helpful.

"Well," I said, "who did?"

He gave the name of a friend of mine living in Houston. I said, "Why, I know him. I didn't know he got your catalog."

John sounded a little hurt. He said, "You know, we do ship all around the country."

"Well, of course, I know you do," I said quickly.

"It's just that when we have something from home that's internationally known, we take it for granted."

He said, "Yeah."

And so I said, "May I ask what's in the package?" All I have to do is hang up, go to the next room, and rip into it.

"I won't tell you," John said. "It's a present. Opening a present is half the fun."

"Well, thank you very much," I told him.

And John said, "Happy New Year."

And I said, "Happy New Year. Good-bye."

I went and opened the package. I found it was a gift that someone had given me in return for a gift that I had given him.

This is how life's presents come too, in a sealed package.

LIFE'S LITTLE PRESENTS

This is how life's presents come too, in a sealed package. And when they come, you say, "Wait a minute. I didn't order this. I'm not so sure I want to look inside, because when I get one of these presents from the Holy Spirit—or life—they aren't always filled with sweet things. Sometimes they've been all pepper. So I think I'd just rather put it off."

You talk to the Inner Master the way I called up John, and you say, "What should I do with this situation that's come into my life?"

The Master says, "Go with it, and see what comes of it."

You say, "Well, I'd rather not. What's this going to lead to?"

The Master says, "Can't tell you. It's a present."

And then you say, "Well, thanks a lot. Happy New Year to you too."

A NEW AGE ILLNESS

For more than a year I've been going through one of the New Age illnesses. It comes from being around too many electronics. This microphone's about the closest I've been to anything electronic for quite a while. It has meant no TV or microwave ovens for months. I stand back if the stove is on. Which is OK. It means I don't have to help with making food too often.

All kinds of things have high electromagnetic radiation. I couldn't believe it. Nothing stops these electromagnetic waves. But there are devices on the market that supposedly neutralize the radiation coming through. And when you're fighting for your health, cost is no object. You spend money on what I call etheric inventions. I asked the seller, "Do they really work? Do you have some kind of test to prove this?" Most of the instruments that are available to the general public aren't sensitive enough to show the effect these devices are having. They said, "Well, plug it in, and see how you feel." I'm not real keen on that because I'm sort of a hard-nosed individual.

With something concrete, you can ask an electrician to check it with a meter. You might say, "The circuit's bad. My speaker isn't working. Could you check it?" The guy brings out a meter, plugs it in, tests a couple of things, and says, "You've got a defective switch."

You say, "OK. How much?" Then he gives you the bill, and you pay it.

But if you tell someone, "My speaker isn't working" and they say, "Well, I've got this bead; you wear it around your neck." Or "I've got this little gadget you can hang around your speaker. Then see how it feels." It just leaves you disgusted. It's hard to have any confidence in this sort of person. "Don't call me; I'll call you," you say.

It's often that way with New Age technology. But there are New Age illnesses that conventional doctors don't know anything about.

HOW DID YOU RECOVER YOUR HEALTH?

I found a catalog that comes out of Syracuse, New York. I'm not here to promote anything, but some of you are familiar with it. It's the *N.E.E.D.S.* catalog. This company sells gadgets, devices, foods, and all sorts of stuff for people who have environmental illnesses.

They also have a newsletter, a bulletin board for their customers. People send in notices like, "I need an Airstream mobile home to live in because I'm having real problems in ordinary houses. I can't live there." Some people are very, very sick from these illnesses.

One time there was a list of items for sale: A totally recovered EI [meaning environmental illness-type person] had an oxygen tank, humidifier, all-glass distiller, car neutralizer, air filter, and things like this for sale.

"Whoa," I said. "This person was really sick! I wonder how she got over it."

I told my wife, "The person lives on the East Coast, but I think I'll give her a call just out of curiosity."

So I called her. "Do you still have some of the items left?" I asked.

"Oh, most are sold. I have a few left."

I said, "Is this your dinner hour?"

She said, "No." Actually, her husband was just finishing up. It was a good time to talk.

There are New Age illnesses that conventional doctors don't know anything about.

I said, "I'm really not interested in your products. But I'm curious. How did you get over this environmental illness? And of all the people who called you asking to buy these products, how many asked what led to your recovery?"

She said, "To answer number two first, nobody ever asked except you."

I thought this was very interesting. We're willing to look at devices and all kinds of stuff to get cures, but when someone we're buying these things from says right there in the ad, "totally recovered," I think the first thing you'd want to do is find out what that person did.

I said, "What happened?" She said she had had a spiritual healing.

Ten years before, she had gotten one of those swine flu shots. It apparently triggered a whole series of reactions in her. And as the years went on, she became more and more sensitive to the chemicals in such things as lawn sprays and perfumes.

It was so bad that if her daughter ran across her neighbor's lawn after they had sprayed, within a day or two this would make the mother very, very sick. She would just get a whiff of something and get sick. She said this had gone on a long time.

She reaffirmed her relationship with the Holy Spirit. Then forgiveness came to her.

Then she got a spiritual healing. She said she reaffirmed her relationship with the Holy Spirit. That was the first thing. Then forgiveness came to her. She, in turn, realized she had to pass this forgiveness on to others.

SPIRITUAL HEALING

It doesn't matter what religion you're in, some people have healings and others don't. Some people in ECK have healings, others don't. Sometimes it's not the fault of the particular Soul, the individual. It can be a necessary life experience.

But other times, when it isn't a necessary life experience or you've learned to love—in this case, she saw it as forgiving herself—a healing can come.

This woman had finally accepted herself spiritually. No more guilt, no more fear.

This is difficult, especially in religions that teach guilt and fear. They say you've got to do this and this and this, and if you don't, then you're going to hell or at least to the warm spots for a certain period of time. It's a little hard to be completely forgiving of yourself under these conditions, and she found it difficult too.

But then she had this forgiveness, and she realized she had to give this forgiveness back to everyone and everything in her life.

This is how she explained it. She said she forgave the fertilizer makers. She forgave the people who made pesticides. After she had had her spiritual healing, she was able to tolerate perfumes right away. It took about two years longer before she could tolerate poisons. She now eats normal foods from the grocery stores, all the regular foods that are chemically treated.

For her, it was realizing that she was a spiritual being and it was OK to just be yourself. She understood this as forgiveness coming to her which she then had to pass along.

When it isn't a necessary life experience or you've learned to love, a healing can come.

HEALING FEAR AND GUILT

It was the most beautiful wisdom. And I pass this along because all of you have come from different faiths before you came to ECK. Most of you have come from the Christian faith. Many have come from other faiths. And if fear and guilt is a part of your upbringing, it can also cause a lot of problems for you in such things as work and in health.

If you can learn to forgive yourself first—and to accept forgiveness—then maybe you can forgive others. And then you can find this healing, because the love of God comes through the Holy Spirit. It is the Holy Spirit.

God exists and speaks to us most directly through the Light and Sound. This is why Eckankar is the Religion of the Light and Sound of God.

It's very popular on television to talk about the Light, but people don't know about the other aspect, the Sound. We have both. This is what makes Eckankar a balanced teaching. In Its fullest sense, this Voice of God is the Holy Spirit. God speaks to us with Its voice—the Holy Spirit—in one way or another.

Often we don't recognize God's help—which usually mean's God's love. We don't recognize it, but other people see it in us.

In Its fullest sense, this Voice of God is the Holy Spirit.

ROSES

An ECKist from the East Coast was coming to Minneapolis for an ECK seminar. He was traveling with another couple. The young man of the couple had just become an ECKist. His wife was very much opposed to ECK but she came along because her husband had promised to take her to the Mall of America.

Sometimes the Holy Spirit works in whatever way It can. It knows our soft spots.

When the wife was on the plane, she began to smell roses. When they landed in Minneapolis–St. Paul, she mentioned it to the ECKist. She said, "I

Sometimes the Holy Spirit works in whatever way It can. It knows our soft spots.

smelled roses, but nobody else could smell them." "Usually this is the sign of the Mahanta, the Living ECK Master," the ECKist said.

The ECK Masters usually have a scent associated with their presence. It's a blessing. It's one of the many kisses of God.

This woman was rather hostile to everything. As they're waiting for baggage, the ECKist—just to make conversation—said to her, "How many ECKists are in your area?" She said, "Seven. Too many." The conversation cooled off a little bit after that.

So they went to the seminar, and over the three-day weekend, the ECKist noticed love entering into this woman. She wasn't even aware of it herself. But divine love began to enter into her. By Sunday morning, she was in the audience early, saving seats, just like she was getting ready for a show at Disney World.

A year later, she came to another seminar in Minneapolis. She was an ECKist by this time. She brought her mother and her sister. She had changed so much. She apologized to the man for the way she had acted the year before.

Before she came to this seminar, she'd seen one of the ECK Masters appear on her couch. "Everything's going to work out all right," he told her.

And this was good for the ECKist she was talking to because he was having his doubts at this time.

He said, "All I want to do is meet one of the ECK Masters one time. Then I would know." Well, maybe his lesson is not to meet an ECK Master. It would be too easy. But the lesson came through a friend who was a great agnostic the year before.

Sometimes when love enters a person, it comes in this way.

The ECK Masters usually have a scent associated with their presence. It's a blessing. It's one of the many kisses of God.

Soul's Tears of Joy

I gave an interview in Australia a couple of years ago, and while we were talking, the interviewer began to cry. I've seen this before, and it's happened to me, coming near the teachings of ECK. Sobs came up inside, and I couldn't understand why. I didn't go in much for that sort of stuff at the time. I held all my emotions in. But it happened to this interviewer, too, in Sydney, Australia.

I just told him, "It's the Holy Spirit bringing God's love to you. That's how it is. That's how it comes."

Master Craftsman

One of the ECKists made the benches for the vestibule of the Temple of ECK. They are beautiful works of art.

As he was working on the benches, the image came to mind that he should sand the underside of the bench too. "Who does that?" he wondered. "All you're going to get on the bottom is some kid's gum. And they have to scratch that off. So why bother? Why make it smooth? Why sand it down?"

Then he remembered this story of an old craftsman. A man came into the shop and saw this old craftsman working under a table. The man said to the craftsman, "What are you doing under the table?"

"I'm sanding a little blemish under here."

"Who will ever know?" the customer said.

And the master craftsman said, "I'll know."

When the person who made these beautiful benches remembered the story, it was the Inner Master talking gently to him, saying, "If you're going to do anything, do it for love or don't do it at all."

So the ECKist began to look at his work in a

If you're going to do anything, do it for love or don't do it at all.

different way. As he thought about it, he realized that the benches were going to be near the staircase and people were going to be able to see the underside of these benches as they went up and down the stairs. And he saw how important it was to take care in everything he did.

RECOGNIZING GOD'S HELP IN YOUR LIFE

Before the 1994 ECK European Seminar in Paris, one of the ECKists was having a lot of lower back and neck pain. She went to doctors; they did a CAT scan, but it looked clear. So they did another CAT scan. This time, they said she had arthritis. She was surprised because the CAT scan looked clear to her and she had experience reading them.

When she went to the seminar in Paris, she noticed that her diet changed. She was eating mostly chicken and vegetables, and she didn't eat as much dessert as usual.

After the seminar was over, she and friends walked around Paris. As she walked all over the city, she realized that her back wasn't hurting her. The pain had been severe, but suddenly neither her back nor her neck was hurting. And she couldn't understand it.

The ECKist came home and went back to work. That day one of her friends mentioned how she doesn't touch any tomatoes, potatoes, chili peppers, or eggplants because they are of the nightshade family. The nightshade family also includes tobacco. It seemed a strange thing to say out of the blue, but the friend explained, "I just thought it was important for you to know this."

The ECKist realized that when she had been in Paris and her back pain went away, she hadn't had any tomatoes, potatoes, or chili peppers. She hadn't

He saw how important it was to take care in everything he did.

been eating any of the nightshades.

This also was God's help in a quiet, gentle way.

*This also
was God's
help in a quiet,
gentle way.*

THE STREET MASTER

At the 1994 ECK Worldwide Seminar in Atlanta, an ECKist, who was an engineering student, had gone out to a restaurant with his sister and brother-in-law after one of the sessions. They took a bus to a very good restaurant, and they had a good evening with stimulating talk.

When it was time to leave the restaurant that evening, the ECKist didn't remember how to get back to his own hotel.

He got some directions from his brother-in-law and started walking back alone. But he got lost, and pretty soon he found himself on a street without lights. In Atlanta there are some dangerous areas, and this was one of them. On one side of the street there were big bushes right next to the sidewalk, and on the other side of the street was a burned-out building.

"I shouldn't be here," the ECKist said.

The Inner Master gave him a nudge, "Don't take another step down this street." So he stood in the middle of the street with his hands in his pockets, just wondering what to do.

He remembered suddenly that at the streetcorner he had bumped into a black man as he came around the corner. So the engineering student hurried back to the corner. "I need help," he said. "I'm going to ask for directions, if I can find someone to ask."

The black man was halfway down the street by now, and the ECKist ran up to him. The man reeked of alcohol, and his eyes were glazed. He seemed to be in a drunken stupor.

"Can you tell me how to get to my hotel?" the

student asked.

The black man turned to him. "Do you know this is a very dangerous place for you?" he said. The student was white.

The student said, "I know. I'm lost."

Just then two men started coming out of the darkness from across the street. The black man waved them away. Probably the signal to them was, "This is my pigeon." But the black man had decided to help this white student find his way out of this very dangerous part of Atlanta.

The two started walking. The black man said, "You shouldn't ever be in a dark street like that. Very, very dangerous. We just got to try to get you out of here now."

And so they walked and walked and walked a long ways. Finally they came within sight of the hotel.

Across the street, there was another black man. He looked like somebody in the business of rolling tourists who come to conventions like this and wander off the beaten path.

The black man said to the white student in a real hearty voice, "Call to that guy across the street, 'Hey, boy!' "

And so the student did. "Hey, boy!" he called. Then he said to the black man, "Isn't that, uh, antagonistic?"

"Only if there's fear in your heart," the man answered.

LOVE WHAT YOU DO

Here was a street master talking to him, telling him how to survive on the street if you get in a place

Here was a street master talking to him, telling him how to survive on the street.

you don't belong. And then the black man said, "I think I'd like to have a cup of coffee."

"Fine," the student said. "Let's go into the coffee shop."

"What are you studying?" the black man asked him.

"I'm in engineering."

"Tell me about it."

The white student rolled his eyes and said to himself, "What is this guy going to understand of engineering?"

Suddenly the black man said to him, "Don't ever be bored with anything you do." This took the student by surprise. He realized that he was bored with engineering. "Life is too short and too precious," the black man said. "Every moment is a blessing. Live life with passion. If you're going to do something, do it with your whole heart."

Then he said, "That street you were on back there. Very dangerous for you." And then he showed the student knife scars on his own body. He said, "See? I've got the scars to prove it. It's dangerous even for me."

They talked for a while. The street master emphasized some of the points that I had made in my talk earlier that evening. He was giving the same points in street language, saying, "This is what you need to do. This is what you must not do if you want to make the most out of this life." The student could then recognize God's help in his life because it was so obvious.

He could have been seriously injured or even killed. But here he was back in his hotel, having coffee with a very interesting man.

> "Life is too short and too precious," the black man said. "Every moment is a blessing. Live life with passion. If you're going to do something, do it with your whole heart."

THE ART OF LISTENING

The man said, "You are a very good listener," which of course is another key to getting on in life.

Instead of talking about everything we know, sometimes it pays to just listen. Listen to the people around you. Because, after all, if someone's telling you something that is spiritual and positive, this is from the Voice of God.

Things that are negative and destructive to you are from the negative side. Do not do them—no matter how spiritual the person is who says to do it.

If someone's telling you something that is spiritual and positive, this is from the Voice of God.

NEW YEAR'S SPIRITUAL EXERCISE

I'd like to give a very short spiritual exercise for those of you who are working on New Year's resolutions.

An ECKist wrote a letter to me and said he had an inner experience with the Inner Master where he was like a prince in his own castle. He lived there in a room. This was a state of consciousness.

As a spiritual exercise, take yourself into a larger room. For example, if you have a desire for self-discipline, like the young dog in the first story, leave the room of self-discipline that you're in. Go down the corridor, and go into another room. This room will be larger. It will be much larger. Just live within the awareness that you want to be in this room of more self-discipline. And then let the Holy Spirit, the ECK, bring about the changes in your life that will accompany such a resolution.

I hope this has helped you. I don't get a chance to speak with you that often. I like to let the ECK initiates address you during worship services throughout the year—at most, I'll take the microphone once or twice a year. There are so many good viewpoints. I'm doing everything possible to let you speak about what you know, because those of you who have the best message to give are often the ones who listen the most to God's voice.

So in this new year, I would like to wish you this blessing of the Vairagi ECK Masters: May the blessings be. My love is with you.

Temple of ECK Worship Service,
Chanhassen, Minnesota, January 1, 1995

In ECK we find that our life is exactly what we have made it sometime in the past. And you are today the very best that you have ever been in any of your past lives. You are the greatest spiritual being you have ever been.

5

WELCOME HOME TO THE TEACHINGS OF ECK

*T*he title for the talk this evening is "Welcome Home to the Teachings of ECK." Those of you who have been in ECK for twenty or twenty-five years are going to say, "What do you mean, welcome home? I am home. These are the teachings I chose years ago."

Other people, here for the first time tonight, are going to say, "What do you mean, welcome home? Taking a little bit for granted, aren't you?"

I have a peculiar ability to get people excited on both ends of the spectrum—without even jumping about the stage and doing a lot of arm waving.

USEFUL TEACHINGS

It's so easy for a spiritual path or a religion to go along the emotional route. The leader whips the people into a frenzy of emotion, and the people then feel that this activity is something spiritually substantial, that it means something, that it has some value. This feeling often lasts just until they get home from church or the meeting. And they have to renew it every week; they've got to go to the battery charger and get their weekly charge.

So much of what passes for truth is a leader playing to the emotions of his followers.

Even if I wanted to wave my arms and say a lot of emotional things to get people all excited—so we would all have a good feeling, go home, and come back again soon—I wouldn't do it. It's my own contract with you and with Divine Spirit to try to give you things that are useful to you spiritually and also practically.

There is no separation between the physical life— your everyday life—and your spiritual life.

MORE THAN PASSIVE ACCEPTANCE

One of the first things you learn on the path of ECK is that there is no separation between the physical life—your everyday life—and your spiritual life. Carrying this a step further, there is no separation between you and the dream world. These are all part of you.

Everything that you are aware of is part of your spiritual life. This includes celebrating one of the holidays because other people around us celebrate it. We do it in our own way. We celebrate our own holidays too.

Having some of the sorrows of life is part of the path of living. The good days and the bad days. We have our celebrations, and we have our sorrows. And so be it.

But what you're expecting out of life is more than the average person expects.

BEST WE'VE EVER BEEN

The average person goes along with everything, almost to the point of passive acceptance of life. Why does someone do that? Why do they just go along with life? *There isn't very much I can do about it,* they think. *No matter what comes up in life, that's just how it is. It's the Lord's will.*

But in ECK we find that our life is exactly what we have made it sometime in the past.

If there is a harsh truth on this path, it's that. You are what you have made yourself. And you are today the very best that you have ever been in any of your past lives.

You may look at yourself and say, "This is the best I've ever been?" And your faith in ECK goes by the wayside. Because we all have images of ourselves as having been great leaders, great kings, great queens at some time in the past. And what are we today? Probably out of work.

So you say, "He's telling me this is the best I've ever been? Why, there were times when thousands would bow down before me or I'd chop their heads off. I remember those times. I saw them in my dreams."

The spiritual path is not about power. It's about love.

LEARNING ABOUT LOVE

But in those ancient days when many of you may have had that kind of power—in some tribe, in some small country—you were learning to deal with power.

And the spiritual path is not about power. It's about love.

When I say that today you are the greatest you've ever been, you are the greatest spiritual being you have ever been. You wouldn't be here if you hadn't learned at least a little about the nature of divine love.

In the past you may have known a whole lot about power. You may still know and exercise and abuse power today. Yes, we do those things. But as we go along, the ECK, or the Holy Spirit, teaches us to do better. How? Through life's experiences.

BLUE LIGHT

Two weeks ago the company that makes M&M candy released a survey they had done. People expressed strong feelings that they should change their tan-colored M&Ms to blue. And so they did, which is nice. And then I understand the Empire State Building put on blue lights to advertise this big change in candy history.

More interesting for some of you is that the color blue is very special in Eckankar. We refer to this as the Blue Light of the Mahanta.

ECK simply means the Holy Spirit. The Holy Spirit is the Voice of God, plain and simple. This Voice of God, the Holy Spirit, has two main ways of being heard and seen: by Sound and by Light. Light and Sound are the two aspects of the Holy Spirit, the ECK.

In your dreams, meditations, or contemplations, you may have seen a light: white, yellow, green, blue, or pink. It can be any color, any shape. It may look like one of the chandeliers up here. It may look like a spotlight. It may look like a candle or a globe.

This is one of the manifestations of the Holy Spirit. Most people don't know what it is, but it's special.

When you see the Light of God, you come out of the experience with a good feeling. You know that the hand of God was near you. And indeed it was, because the Voice of God has brought the gift of God's love to you.

SOUNDS OF GOD

The second way that the Holy Spirit communicates with people is through the Sound. Again, the Sound of God can be any number of different sounds.

Light and Sound are the two aspects of the Holy Spirit, the ECK.

When you see the Light of God, you come out of the experience with a good feeling. You know that the hand of God was near you.

In contemplation or meditation, you may hear a high humming sound. It may be a sound like bees swarming around their hive. It can be the sound of running water. It can be the sound of a flute. It can be the sound of a whistle. It can be the sound of distant bells. Or the sound of the ocean or singing birds.

These are all sounds of the Holy Spirit coming through at a particular level, coming to you at your state of consciousness at that time. And this uplifts you spiritually. If at any time in your life you've experienced these two aspects of the Holy Spirit, it's a way that God's love was coming through to you.

We're told in some of our human scriptures that God's love is basically an indefinable thing. It's a feeling, more or less. But we in ECK say that you can see it and you can hear it.

When this divine love comes into you, it will change you. It changes your state of consciousness.

And when this divine love comes into you, it will change you. It changes your state of consciousness. Degree by degree, it makes you a new person. A lot of times you wonder what's going on, what's happening. You have no idea. And then one day, you come across the teachings of ECK, and you say, "Oh, this makes sense."

GIVING OTHERS FREE CHOICE

Maybe you stay with the teachings of ECK for a year or two. Then you say, "It doesn't make sense anymore," and leave. You won't find anybody chasing you, trying to reconvert you. At least they shouldn't be.

I don't try to hold people who want to leave ECK. I don't try to stop people from coming to ECK either, unless I can see that they're not spiritually ready. If you try to hold someone against their will—even to a religious or spiritual path—you limit your own freedom.

I come from a country background. If cattle were fenced in and didn't want to stay there and the fence wasn't good, a farmer would spend a lot of time watching those cattle to make sure that they didn't break out and get into the next pasture. If they were in a pasture that was grazed down and the next field was a field of oats, you could bet that they were going to test your fence every chance they got.

It's that way too, trying to hold someone who doesn't want to be on the path that you are on.

They know that the grass is greener on the other side of the fence. So let them go. If you let them go, you don't waste a lot of energy. It's not like a farmer who has to fix the fence and keep the cattle out of the oat field because he'll lose productivity. If a person wants to go follow his own path, let him go. What's it to you?

It's that person's free choice, as it should be. After all, you have free choice too, to follow your own path.

You have free choice to follow your own path.

DISGUISES

I was looking in an Eckankar brochure and saw a photo of myself without glasses. Here I am wearing them again.

One of my favorite television shows when I was still watching was *'Allo, 'Allo.* This is a British comedy about World War II in France. The French owner of a café has a number of employees working there, and of course they're with the French underground.

One of the characters is the old piano player. He would always come sneaking into the restaurant in one of his disguises. But no matter what disguise he put on, he always looked the same.

He'd come into the restaurant, look around very

carefully to see if the enemy soldiers had recognized him, then go up to René, the café owner. He'd raise his glasses—so René could see behind his clever disguise—and he'd say, "It is I, Leclerc." And René would always be so frustrated. He'd say, "Of course, you fool, who else would it be?"

Well, it is I, Leclerc.

COMMON GROUND

One of the benefits of being in Eckankar is often overlooked: simply being with a group of people who have had experiences in life that are not ordinary or commonplace. Experiences with the Light and Sound of ECK.

You've become familiar with a lot of different experiences and have insights into life that the average person does not have. And so you can talk about things with each other that people outside of ECK would consider on the far side. But these are some of the facts of life.

I find it interesting that often people outside of ECK have such a limited view of life. And this view of life is a perfect reflection of their own state of consciousness.

If someone's narrow-minded, his view of life is going to be very narrow-minded. And so on. Even some of the most broad-minded people—we find them as leaders in religion and politics—don't understand the Law of Cause and Effect. What are the causes that drive life here? What are the responsibilities that a Soul has in this life? If our leaders understood the spiritual Law of Cause and Effect, they would be making entirely different decisions, especially if they knew they are accountable for their actions in government.

One of the benefits of being in Eckankar is being with a group of people who have had experiences in life that are not ordinary or commonplace. Experiences with the Light and Sound of ECK.

PERFECT ACCOUNTABILITY

ECK is a teaching of perfect accountability for everything we do, for everything that comes into our life, for everything that we expect to come into our life in the future. We realize that we must take full responsibility for everything we do.

For instance when we're sick, usually the first thing we say is, "It's someone else's fault," or "It's a psychic attack from someone."And why not? Relieves us of responsibility. We usually don't say, "I'm sick because of something I did." We say, "Somebody else, over there in the shadows, is shooting psychic arrows at me. Boy, will life get him." And that's our way out of accepting responsibility for ourselves.

But when we move into new areas of consciousness, we find that our whole life must change around us. We have to live by new rules.

Truth means meeting yourself.

WHAT IS TRUTH?

Those of you who have moved through several different levels of spiritual consciousness have found that your life can get rough at times. Why? Not because somebody in the dark alley is shooting arrows at you. It's because you're meeting yourself.And this is truth. Truth means meeting yourself.

It's one of the paradoxes of truth. So many people claim to have truth. So many people claim to know it. But they can't agree with each other about what truth is. And they're ready to fight to the death to have their view of truth prevail.

This is wrong. Because if you have truth, you realize that another person has truth too, at his or her own level. There's no reason to fight about it.

As sure as you're alive, if you can make it over

the next hurdle, through the next stormy sea, your view of life will change. And so will your viewpoint on truth. Why? Because the experience made you wiser. You will have a broader view of truth.

This is why we in ECK don't go looking for trouble. We don't say, "I want troubles so that I shall become wiser and more spiritual." No. If you're wise and if you're spiritual, you'll do everything possible to live a smooth, calm, peaceful life.

Because it's more harmonious. That's our goal.

But in ECK, we find that when we move into a higher state of consciousness, things do get rough for a while. We work off our limited states of consciousness so that we can live and move in greater states. And the greater states of consciousness mean more freedom to live, move, and do as we wish.

The greater states of consciousness mean more freedom to live, move, and do as we wish.

Wake-Up Call

An ECK family has a dog. And when they came to the seminar, they had to put the dog in a kennel. They have some cats too, but the cats are very self-sufficient. The family can leave them food and water and put them in a room, and they'll be OK. Cats are survivors. But a dog is better off at a kennel. Dogs need a different kind of care and attention.

When the family is at home, this young dog has a certain habit. She sleeps all night, very patiently. Then early in the morning at six o'clock, the dog barks once.

The bark means, "It's been a long night, and I've got to go outside. Now!"

If the master wants to sleep a little bit longer because it's Saturday or Sunday morning, the dog barks one more time—not very loud, but loud enough.

During the seminar, the dog was in the kennel,

and the master was hundreds of miles away from home. The first morning of the seminar, at six o'clock, the man was sleeping when suddenly he heard the bark of his dog, loud and clear, "It's time to get up."

He opened his eyes, thinking he was home. But he was in a hotel room.

And then he realized that across the miles, the dog had actually said, "Good morning. I'm thinking of you. I hope somebody takes care of me now. I've got to go outside."

A BOND OF LOVE

What binds people, animals, and all beings together in this world and in the other worlds? Simply divine love. When the dog barks and the master hears it, even though they're separated by miles, this is a bond of love.

Sometimes on the radio, I hear people talking at great length about how animals don't have any awareness. You just want to change the station when someone says, "Animals don't have a state of consciousness. They don't know what's going on." Yes, there are some very stupid animals. There are also some very stupid people. But on the other hand, there are also some very intelligent cats and dogs as well as very intelligent people.

Where the state of consciousness is high in a Soul—whether It has taken the form of a human being, a cat, or a dog—there is this bond of love.

Some people don't believe in a state of consciousness for animals. These are the people who feel that God's love is limited to human beings. If these same people were living in the Middle Ages, they would be the ones who'd say, "God's love is limited to earth. Therefore, earth is the center of the universe." This

Where the state of consciousness is high in a Soul— whether It has taken the form of a human being, a cat, or a dog—there is this bond of love.

is the sort of thinking that we laugh at today.

In the future, some clever scientist will come up with some way to prove that animals and people are more than just the mind. There's something beyond the mind. The animating feature in a living being is not the mind but Soul.

And what is Soul? It is you, the real being.

SOUL IS THE REAL YOU

One of the wrong ideas that people have before coming to ECK is, "I have a Soul." Who's this *I* speaking? The *I* that's speaking is you. That is Soul. Whenever you say, "I have a Soul," wrong thinking comes in. You cannot possess or own Soul. Soul in Its natural, high state is free. Who's this human being saying, "I have a Soul?"

At death the human body decays. Soul—the real part—lives forever.

It's funny. People without the knowledge of Divine Spirit put this peculiar twist on the nature of Soul. In their mortal bodies they say, "I have a Soul." But they're speaking as immortal Soul without knowing it.

The mortal part of them says, "I have a Soul." The mortal part likes to possess, to own. The immortal part—Soul—does not like to possess or own. It simply wants to bathe in the love and mercy of God. Soul is content to do that and to serve God out of gratitude and thankfulness. That's why the theme of this seminar is "The Grateful Heart."

THE GREATEST BLESSING

We serve God and life out of gratitude. Why? For the blessings we have received.

At death the human body decays. Soul— the real part— lives forever.

And what is the greatest blessing? The gift of life itself. Just to be able to come to a seminar such as this —to travel here, to go through all the different rigors that many of you have gone through just to get here — this is part of the blessing of life. It's living. It's getting more experience in life, learning more about who and what you are. What else is life than that?

The more you learn about yourself, the more you have to give back to life. It's natural. You have to. Your heart opens, you have greater capacity for love. To get more love, you have to give more love. As you give more, you get more.

The more you learn about yourself, the more you have to give back to life.

CHILD'S AWARENESS

At the age of four or five, children are still in touch with Divine Spirit, the Holy Spirit. Then the influence of school comes upon them, and pretty soon they become numb. They have to learn all the right ways to study, watch TV, play computer games — and all this slowly comes in and closes them down. It closes down the spiritual consciousness of a lot of people. And it's not a bad thing because it's the nature of life.

Children at an early age often remember past lives, and they'll tell you about them, if you're their parent. Just ask them a question like, What were you last time when you were big? They'll come up with some very interesting answers. And if you just listen and make believe you are the child listening to a great sage, you can learn a lot from children.

Children have the wisdom of God and are closer to it than many people who have spent years in this world gaining all kinds of knowledge about the nature of religion. Children have it naturally.

WHERE DO WORDS COME FROM?

One evening, a child asked his mother, "Where do words come from?"

The mother was at the end of a hard day. She was making dinner for the family, and her mind was on some things that had gone on at work and with her husband.

Kids can come up with some good questions. "That's a hard one to answer," she said. But the little boy didn't care.

He said, "Words were here before there were dinosaurs."

"There weren't people when there were dinosaurs."

"Before there were people and dinosaurs, there were words," he said. He didn't ask. He told her.

So she said, "I suppose words could come from dreams and the HU."

And the boy said, "That's a good answer, Mommy." He spoke with a surety about some of the truths of where things in this world originated, even things as basic as language.

We take language for granted. Where do words come from? Our anthropologists would probably run to Africa and trace the genetic tree of one group or another, then make all kinds of suppositions about what point people left off grunting. A certain grunt meant, "Hit the animal." They would ask each other, "What does this grunt mean?" and so on. But it never occurs to people that much of the early information about language came to people from the dream state.

This teaching came through the Holy Spirit, working through its messengers, the ECK Masters. Children know. At least some children know. At least this child knew.

Much of the early information about language came to people from the dream state.

GOOD THINGS

As time passes we find that we live more and more in an information age—computers talking back and forth across the world very quickly on the Internet. Languages that existed for centuries in small pockets in remote areas of the world are dying out. Some people are very upset about this.

These are the same people who are upset when a forgotten tribe is discovered in South America. They go down there to save the people from the intrusions of the twentieth century. Well, the people there like the intrusions of the twentieth century. They like them as much as the anthropologists do. They like record players and CDs. This worries the anthropologists. They say, "Oh, but if you get record players, then you're going to lose your ancient songs."

The people say, "We don't care. We want records and stuff. We want CDs."

The anthropologists say, "But it will ruin you." And when the anthropologist finishes his tour, he flies back home to the States, gets to his apartment, turns on a CD player, and says, "Boy, that's a sad thing; we're losing a culture that will never be here again." But those people like the twentieth century too.

Some people want to hold on to good things for themselves yet prevent others from having them.

WHEN TO LET THINGS BE

That's the funny thing about some people. They want to hold on to good things for themselves yet prevent others from having them.

Sometimes I get a kick out of certain groups. They're always saving Montana or some other place, but most of the people who are saving those remote places live elsewhere—in Colorado, California, or New York. They should go home and save New York

City. But that's just my opinion.

You see, when we try to save cultures, we're really trying to exercise power upon other people. And this is still a sign of someone who is not as spiritually advanced as he or she thinks. If you're willing to let things be, sometimes it's better.

I'm not talking about atrocities, such as genocide. I feel that people with spiritual awareness have a duty to protect those who cannot protect themselves.

But you have to understand something first: do these people want protection?

Do they want to save their lives but not have the means to do so? Are they willing to be responsible and not take the law into their own hands as soon as they get help? Or are they going to then go slaughter the other side as freely as the other side tried to slaughter them? You don't want to help people like that. The people in former Yugoslavia have been after each other for a thousand years. And we stepped into the middle of this.

An Exercise in Power

These people, for whatever reasons, want to do each other in. You give a little advantage to one side, and instead of trying to make peace with it, they try to extinguish their enemies. And if their enemies get a little bit of power, they try to do the same.

An exercise in power: This is basically what this earth is about. Political and religious leaders think they're doing good when they try to keep people from themselves. In some cases, it's best to simply withdraw and get out of the fighter's ring. Don't be near it if you have a choice.

These people are working out heavy karmic debts. Through the Law of Reincarnation they've been

An exercise in power: This is basically what this earth is about.

working them out for centuries, even as people in other parts of the world are working out their karmic debts with each other. Do what you can—but you make better decisions about what to do or what not to do if you have an understanding of the Law of Cause and Effect.

People are responsible for what they do. But on the other hand, sometimes you have to leave people alone to learn their own lessons.

FIGURING OUT CAUSE AND EFFECT

At the ECK Worldwide Seminar in Atlanta last year, I talked about health. I try to talk about health in a general way, so that those of you who have the awareness can pick up something and take it a step beyond what I said. I can speak about my own health conditions, but as far as you're concerned, so what? If you're younger, you may not have health conditions, or if you're older and in good health, you may say, "Well, this is all useless."

But I try to point out certain things, so that people at least have an idea about how to figure out the cause and effect in their lives. And as Divine Spirit gives them one answer, they can then take it a step further.

They can work their way to their own solution. They can find some remedy for their illness, if this is to be in their life.

I try to point out certain things, so that people at least have an idea about how to figure out the cause and effect in their lives.

TERMITES

A woman wrote me a letter. In the past, she had had asthma—a very bad case of it. But she had been free of it for three years. After the Atlanta seminar, she went back home. She lives in a very humid area of the country. As soon as she got home, the asthma came back. It became a fight for breath, just trying to stay alive.

She went to a number of doctors. One said, "Cut out certain foods that you have shown an allergy to in the past." She did that. It didn't work. Another said, "Here's some medication. Take it. Maybe it will help." It didn't help. And she was at a loss as to what was causing the return of her condition.

She had been to a number of different doctors trying to get help. About this time she found that the house she had lived in for eighteen and a half years had termites.

Sometimes the house is a waking-dream symbol for our physical body.

Sometimes the house is a waking-dream symbol for our physical body. "Termites," she said. "OK, what do I do to get rid of the termites?" It means getting people in to exterminate them. And of course they use strong poisons.

The woman contacted a few of her doctors. "What happens if they use these poisons on my house to kill the termites? What's going to happen to me?" she asked. Some people are very sensitive to these poisons.

The doctors said that, considering her condition, it probably wouldn't be very good for her.

A friend of hers who is a housing inspector happened to stop by about this time. He was going to look at the termite problem one more time. So he checked around her home. When he came to the air conditioner, he saw that the air-exchange unit was loaded with mildew.

People who have environmental illnesses are often very sensitive to mold and mildew. The woman discovered that the mildew was causing the recurrence of her asthma attack. She moved in with relatives.

A letter of thanks came to me not long after.

"Thank you for sending the termites," she wrote. "Because of them, somebody found out that my home had mildew. And the mildew was causing my asthma." So the steps were from termites to mildew to asthma.

ENVIRONMENTAL ILLNESS

There's a lot of energy flowing into our homes. And some people are genetically not strong enough to withstand the high levels of electromagnetic radiation.

A lot of medical doctors can't make the connection between symptoms and the new environmental illnesses that are coming out today. Many of the symptoms are the same as for arthritis, asthma, or some other illness. But the doctors are not seeing the connection with environmental illnesses.

As our society gets more advanced in technology, new homes have more and more electrical wiring. Why? Because the extra wiring is necessary to support VCRs, two TVs, three TVs, four TVs, CD systems, and microwave ovens — all the different appliances we depend on. There's a lot of energy flowing into our homes. And some people are genetically not strong enough to withstand the high levels of electromagnetic radiation. Magnetism comes from the earth too. But it is of a different and weaker kind.

Some people find that their environmental illness takes the form I experienced — sensitivity to electromagnetic radiation. I'm not watching any television. I know where the cool places in our home are because I have a meter. I've checked out our home.

Sometimes the radiation levels are very high. For instance, around dinner hour, the electric companies pump out more electricity because people are going to be using more to cook dinner. And those of you who are sensitive may not feel real well around that time. Gradually you may find yourself becoming a little less able than you were before. But there are ways around all of this. I'm working on it now, and if I figure it out, I'll let you know.

A Simple Problem

A family built a yurt out on an island in the St. Lawrence River. A yurt is a semipermanent home that Mongols and other nomadic people used to use. It can take all forms. It can be a round structure, and you stretch tent material over it. This man's family sometimes sleeps in the yurt. It's living close to nature, and it's good for them. There's something healthy about this; it gets them close to earth's magnetic currents —the natural ones —and far away from some of the unnatural ones that are bombarding us.

But this family's immediate problem wasn't electromagnetic radiation. It was something simpler: raccoons.

They had a little kitchen attached to this yurt, and the raccoons wanted to get at the food. And trying to get to the food, they would damage the yurt. The father tried a number of different things to solve the problem.

First, he chased the raccoons away from the yurt, just as I did at one home I lived in. The raccoons would get into my flower beds at night. I had some potatoes in the refrigerator. I said, "This ought to fix them." So I threw the potatoes at them. I hit them, but they didn't care. They ate the potatoes. So I told my wife, "That didn't do any good, except that I got those old potatoes out of the refrigerator." But the raccoons didn't go away.

This family found the same thing. Each time the father chased the raccoons, they came back, and they would go straight for the kitchen.

So then he took a little BB gun, and he buzzed

them with it. The raccoons were annoyed, but it takes a lot more than annoyance to discourage a raccoon who is trying to get to food.

The father didn't know what else to do. So one day he went up on a ridge that was very close to the raccoons' den. And he sang a song to them.

Before he began his song, he chanted HU. He chanted HU first because he wanted to talk to these animals. He wanted to get a message across. Then he sang his song. It basically said: "Hey, you guys, you're invading the privacy of myself and my family. How would you like it if we came over into your den and violated your freedom? Do you think you'd like that?"

And so he sang this way for a little while. Then he sang to the raccoons, "You want your freedom, and you want respect for your home. I want freedom, and I want respect for my home too." After he finished that song, he ended by singing HU. He began with HU, and he ended with HU.

For a little while, this worked. The man was very happy that the raccoons had respected his wish. But knowing raccoons, I wouldn't be surprised if he saw them again because they have short memories. Very much the same as some of us do.

We make our New Year's resolutions, and before April, we've forgotten them. But it's OK. Maybe we'll make them again next year, and maybe we'll have more luck in keeping them.

A Spiritual Dream

One person had a spiritual dream. In the dream he was working for a very important person who was running a company. The dreamer's job was to take four pairs of shoes—the very best athletic shoes in the world—to a large football stadium.

It was supposed to be a big event. Even the playing field had been set up with chairs. But only four people came. Here he had four pair of shoes, and there were only four people. The dreamer was thinking, *It doesn't look like we're going to get a lot of promotional advantage out of these four pair of shoes with only four people.*

One of the people was a professional football player. The professional football player represented someone who is a truth seeker—because he has trained and disciplined himself. He got a pair of shoes.

A very large man was seated in the lower level of the stadium near the balcony. He wasn't a football player, but he was a truth seeker of the same sort as the football player. In the dream, the large man represented a large heart, a great capacity to love. Life had taught him the disciplines that the football player had picked up in training camp. He got a pair of shoes.

Another person was sitting very close to the dreamer, so he got a pair of shoes. And off at the other end, there was a guy sitting all by himself. He had just happened to wander in. He didn't really belong there. He wasn't real interested in football. He wasn't athletic. Nothing.

The dreamer was holding the last pair of shoes. He was standing with the football player.

"There should have been thousands of professional football players here today," the man said to the football player—meaning thousands of truth seekers, people who had the self-discipline to follow the path to God. "But," he says, "they must not care. Nobody's come."

Just then, the back door opened, and into this stadium came all these professional football players—

thousands of them. And they just kept filing in until they filled up the whole place, the playing field, the lower level, and the balcony.

The dreamer has another problem now. He's got only one pair of shoes left, and it's got to go to absolutely the best person in the stadium. It was a tough decision.

The man decided he wouldn't give the shoes to the person who had just wandered in; the person obviously didn't care. So he asked the football player beside him. He said, "Who is the very best player here, the most worthy of this exceptional pair of shoes?" They were really good shoes. You could run faster, turn better, and do all those things.

And the football player said, "There's a quarterback over there." The quarterback is the one who runs the team, and this quarterback was the star of the winning team. "I think that quarterback would be the best person to give these shoes to." The quarterback was seated just a few seats up. So the dreamer gave the last pair of shoes to the quarterback.

What are the shoes? Shoes in dreams generally mean a way of travel—how to get from one place to another, like the teachings of ECK. It is a means, a mode of accomplishing something. In American football, as in a lot of other games, there's a goal and a way to get to the goal through intermediate stages. You have to accomplish something in American football. You have to get the first down. If you get the first down, then you go a little bit farther. Eventually, if you drive hard enough and you're good enough, you make a touchdown.

The teachings of ECK are here. And they're being given out in different ways to different people.

This was a very spiritual dream. It meant that the teachings of ECK are here. And they're being given out in different ways to different people.

Some have appreciated and have been worthy of the ECK teachings. Others just fell into them, if you will. Others were born into them. They don't understand the value of the teachings. But I have a feeling there are a lot of people yet to come who will understand and appreciate the ECK teachings as the voice of truth.

WELCOME HOME TO THE TEACHINGS OF ECK

One of the members of ECK is a hospice worker. One day she got an emergency call. Could she fill in for the regular hospice worker who was scheduled to visit a woman dying of cancer?

So the hospice worker went to the woman's home. The dying woman's daughter was there for a little bit. And then she left. She had to run some errands. So it was just the ECKist and this woman who was dying of cancer. So they talked for a while.

After some time, the hospice worker noticed that the woman appeared to be very distressed. So she asked, "Are you in pain?"

The woman said no. They talked a little bit more, but this look of distress stayed on the woman's face. So the hospice worker said, "Could I call a minister of your faith for you? Would you like to talk to a minister?"

And again the woman said no.

Then the woman spoke what was in her heart. "Many years ago, I was in Las Vegas," she said. "I went to a place called Eckankar. The people there were very kind and good. And in this ECK center, there were pictures on the wall of men I had met in my dreams. And the people said things to me that I didn't understand. But I felt good there. When I

There are a lot of people yet to come who will understand and appreciate the ECK teachings as the voice of truth.

went home, I brought some ECK books with me."
She'd ordered some more, she said, but her husband
felt she shouldn't be looking into things like that. He
burned her ECK books. And so for years, this woman
who had made this connection with ECK was again
cut off, and now she was ending this life.

The ECKist said to her, "I am an ECKist."

The woman said, "This means everything in the
world to me. I've waited so long."

The ECKist said, "Would you like to sing HU
together?"

And the woman said she'd very much like to.

So they sang HU for about five minutes. They
shut their eyes, and they sang this love song to God.
At the end of that time, the ECKist said to the patient,
"Did you see anything?"

The sick woman said, "Yes, a man came to me and
said, 'Don't be afraid.'" And the woman talked about
her experiences with the Light and Sound. She wanted
to know what they were. And so they passed several
more hours in this way until the daughter came home.
Before the hospice worker left, she said, "Always
remember you're not alone."

The dying woman said, "I know that now."

A connection was made twenty-five years ago
when the Eckankar headquarters was in Las Vegas.
The seeker had found ECK, but then through circumstances of karma with her husband in this lifetime,
she had lost it again. He burned her books and for-
bade her to study Eckankar. But more than likely
when she leaves this lifetime, she will come back into
another situation — either into an ECK family or into
circumstances where it will be possible for her to get
close to the ECK teachings again when she comes of
age.

Always remember you're not alone.

I thank you for coming, and I'll leave you with the blessing of the Vairagi Order. May the blessings be.

ECK Springtime Seminar, New York, New York,
Friday, April 14, 1995

The inner teachings are the greater part of the ECK teachings. The Inner Master can meet you in your dreams and speak to each one of you directly and give you exactly the spiritual help that you need.

6

WALK WITH ME, MAHANTA

I'd like to welcome those of you who are new to Eckankar. A man came to the talk for the first time last night, and later he said that the message was directly for him. And so he was coming back tonight.

The talk title for this evening is "Walk with Me, Mahanta." I'd like to explain the term *Mahanta*.

WHAT IS THE MAHANTA?

Eckankar has two parts: the inner and the outer teachings. The outer teachings include talks, books, and discourses and the *Mystic World* for those who become members of Eckankar. But the inner teachings are the greater part of this path: dreams and dream travel, Soul Travel, and the ECK-Vidya— getting an insight in contemplation into your own future or other things that are helpful to you if and when the occasion warrants.

There are also the two parts of the Master: the Outer Master and the Inner Master. During my talks and through my writings, I work in the role of the Outer Master where I give you what I can.

Eckankar has two parts: the inner and the outer teachings.

I am all too aware of my limitations. Sometimes I go back to the hotel room after a talk and tell my wife, "I wish I were able to say things better and more clearly so that people would be able to take the very most spiritual benefit back home with them."

But the greater part of this teaching is the Inner Master, the Mahanta. It's a state of consciousness. It is my inner side.

Working with Divine Spirit, this inner form is something that you can see inwardly as the Inner Master. Each one of you can see it individually at some time or another. Some of you may see the Inner Master. Some of you may see other ECK Masters. You may see the Light of God, you may hear the Sound of God. Anything of this nature is very good for you spiritually.

The inner teachings are custom fitted for each one of you individually.

FITTING THE ECK TEACHINGS TO YOU

The inner teachings are custom fitted for each one of you individually. The outer teachings cannot be.

I sit at my desk, and I write articles and letters. But I have to address you as a group, a group consciousness. In other words, I have to find the pulse, where the spirit of the ECK students is today, and then speak to you in that way.

It works pretty well. But nothing beats the Inner Master.

The Inner Master can meet you in your dreams and speak to each one of you directly and give you exactly the spiritual help that you need.

For some, these are preposterous statements. That anyone would say there is such a thing going on in the world today. But it does happen. In my talks, I tell stories about people who have come in contact with the ECK Masters and benefited spiritually.

Whether or not someone believes this depends upon their own experience. Their own experience is what helps them move forward spiritually. Or sometimes it holds them back—if they won't throw away the unnecessary karmic baggage or habits that hold them back, like anger. Then they don't move forward as quickly as they'd like. And then, of course, the Inner and the Outer Master both get credit for that.

Their own experience is what helps them move forward spiritually.

But I'm used to it. It's just part of this position. I realize that, at some point, people will get a little further along the spiritual path and understand that the responsibility for their spiritual unfoldment begins and ends with themselves. So I don't worry about it.

Some people come to ECK, and they leave ECK. It's just how life is. Because here in the lower worlds, anything that has a beginning also has an ending. It's the nature of life here. This applies to everything, whether it's a job or a relationship. We don't like to think about endings, especially if we're in a happy relationship. But the truth of this world is: anything that begins will someday end.

THE OLDEST MAN IN THE WORLD

A couple of weeks ago, the oldest man in the world died at the age of 147. I think he was from China; he lived a very simple life. He was a peasant. And he ate mostly rice and corn. People in our society say you have to eat a varied, balanced diet—otherwise, you don't live very long. But this guy did OK for having just rice and corn most of his life. It got me thinking.

Probably what made him live so long was not the nutrition from rice and corn. The strength of his diet was moderation. If that's all you ate every day, you'd eat just as much as you had to just to stay alive, I would guess. If you see rice every day, you just eat what you have to. "Corn again? OK." Shovel it down. Go out and work again.

If you're going to live to be 147 years old, you're going to have a lot of joy in your life simply because you put in so much time. But there are also going to be many unhappy times.

When life dishes it out to us, try to take it in stride.

A man like this must have learned how to roll with life. When things went wrong, he learned how to take it in stride.

This is an important lesson that we can all learn from the oldest person in the world: When life dishes it out to us, try to take it in stride. I know it's difficult when we have losses that are very close to us. It can be very hard to deal with. But we do the best we can. And we try to be in harmony with the currents of life. We try not to get too upset about things when they go wrong.

This is the lesson we can learn from this man who lived to be 147. It's more than just the little news item coming across the radio or TV, told in passing by a news commentator.

ECK MASTER WITH NO NAME

One of the ECKists works with the dream state. And in his dreams, he kept meeting this Master.

He wanted to know the Master's name. But in the dream when he asked the different people he met, "Who is that ECK Master?" the best anyone could tell him was. "That's the ECK Master with no name."

One night, this Master came to him in a dream. By now the dreamer wasn't sure if this was a good spirit or a bad spirit. But we have a test in the teachings of ECK. We sing the word *HU,* which is a love song to God, and we see whether this entity or person can stay or if this makes the person go away.

As soon as the dreamer began to chant HU, this Master with no name began to chant HU with him. After they finished, the ECK Master said, "It's a pretty sound, isn't it?" He said it like he was totally in harmony with HU.

And so the dreamer knew he was one of the ECK Masters, one of the high spiritual beings who come to help people.

IN TUNE WITH TODAY

Then the Master without a name took the dreamer to a future ECK seminar. And how far in the future was it? In 1995, we released Mahanta Transcripts, Book 10, the tenth year of my talks. In the dream, the ECKist went into the seminar bookroom and saw Mahanta Transcripts, Book 34, 35, 36, and beyond. He did some quick arithmetic and discovered they were in the year 2021.

The dreamer wanted to read these future Mahanta Transcripts now, but he knew he couldn't. And the ECK Master with him said, "The truth in the Mahanta Transcripts is given out for the times in which they are released. To go into the future, read these books, and then try to apply their truths in the present time would be a mistake. You might feel that some of this information from the future applies today, but it doesn't."

One of the benefits and strengths of Eckankar is that it constantly keeps up with the changing consciousness of people today. In other words, you cannot have old scriptures as your sole message to people.

One of the benefits and strengths of Eckankar is that it constantly keeps up with the changing consciousness of people today.

What people could understand and accept in medieval times is entirely primitive if you compare it to what people can understand and accept today. Those were the Dark Ages. People's understanding about life and God was entirely different from today.

The teachings of ECK have to stay in tune—stay in step—with the consciousness of the people if the teachings are to be effective. And the ECK teachings do this. So that whatever we are releasing today is what people today can accept and understand. In five, ten, fifteen, or twenty years, the teachings will be different. They will be broader. Each time, truth takes another step and broadens.

CROOKED ROAD

Out in the country where I grew up, there was this crooked road. It went straight north, then for no apparent reason it went west for a quarter of a mile. Then it went north again for another half mile or so, and it kind of wound around until it ended up at a major highway. I often wondered about this, and I asked my father about it. He said it used to be an old Indian trail. When his father was a young boy, Indians used to travel that trail. But they hadn't for years.

And so I wondered about this. Suddenly it was as if I were in the past as an Indian boy walking that trail, seeing all those white people come in. Suddenly my world wasn't the same anymore. And it felt as if I didn't belong there.

The same thing happened in this lifetime. There used to be farms along that crooked road. When I went back a few years ago, there were houses where the fields used to be. Where we used to bale hay and load grain for threshing, where I would help neighbors work, were now rows of houses. And suddenly, I had no interest in the land anymore. I said, "That may have been where I grew up, but there's nothing there for me anymore."

Some initiates in ECK who came in at a certain time now feel as if the path has gone wrong. Whenever they came to the path, they feel that time was the beginning of the true teachings. Because that was the point when they found the true teachings. Then the teachings expand and expand, and the people are stretched like rubber bands. They come to the very limits of how far they can go in this lifetime. And when they come to that limit, they will say, "Nope. This path is now going wrong."

Most people won't leave. But the ones that do never think of looking around at others who came in at the same point they did. These people never ask, "Are the others all leaving?" They're not leaving.

So then what's the problem? The problem is the individual's state of consciousness. He's frozen into a little space like an egg. And when changes try to push him beyond that little space, he can't go. He feels uncomfortable, and often he leaves with a lot of anger, only to come back in another life a little bit more humble, a little wiser because the experiences of life have made him so.

"Walk with Me, Mahanta" means that you have this inner part of the Master with you at all times.

THE MASTER IS ALWAYS WITH YOU

"Walk with Me, Mahanta" means that you have this inner part of the Master with you at all times. Some people say, "I call the Master, and then the Master comes." That's not quite true; the Master is always with you.

Inwardly, I am always with you. I am with you now. I am with you outwardly here in the room at this seminar. But, two or three weeks from now, when you are home, sometimes things happen. You're back at work. Things are difficult. You feel so cut off from life and love and everything else that matters. But then you say, "Wait a minute. Maybe if I sing HU, the Mahanta will come." And so then you sing HU, and all of a sudden you become aware of the presence of the Mahanta.

But you may mistake this for the Mahanta coming. You don't realize the Mahanta was always there.

When the spiritual student begins to sing HU, he opens his consciousness to recognize the presence of the Master. The Inner Master is always with you. He is *always* with you.

The Inner Master is always with you. He is always with you.

SOUL'S TRUE FOOD

A man from Africa had a drinking problem. He drank a lot of beer. As far as he was concerned, beer was food for him. It was food for body and Soul. His relatives thought he was possessed by entities, maybe around ten of them. They said to each other, "This guy drinks a lot. He must have someone helping him."

When the man came into ECK, he said, "I've got to get rid of this habit. I don't need beer anymore." But it was difficult, because he'd had the habit for such a long time. He didn't know how to get rid of it.

So he asked the Mahanta in contemplation, "Please help me break this habit. I now have the true food for body and Soul." He had food for Soul. For the body, you still need physical food, the corn and the rice.

True food for Soul is the Light and Sound of God, the two parts of the Holy Spirit.

True food for Soul is the Light and Sound of God, the two parts of the Holy Spirit. ECK equals the Holy Spirit which equals the Light and Sound which equals divine love. These things are all one and the same. When we try to explain what this or that part of it is, it's very difficult. Basically, the Light and Sound of God are divine love coming into your life. It's that and nothing more.

One night the African man had a dream. He found himself in front of a large office building. As he walked to the door, he was carrying a five-liter container of beer. He was there to pick up a package. But before he could go into the office, he had to leave his five liters of beer outside. So he went into the office, opened a desk drawer, and saw the package that he was there to collect.

The man took the package, left the office, and forgot all about his five-liter container of beer. As he was walking home in his dream, right before he reached his front gate, a dove flew down as if it wanted to land on his shoulder. A dove is one of the signs of the Holy Spirit, as it is in Christianity— when Jesus was coming out of the water at his baptism, there was the dove.

But this new member of ECK was trying to get off his habit of beer. He just waved and said, "Thank you," because he recognized why the dove was there. It was a blessing.

The dove flew off. The ECKist looked toward the gate of his home that enclosed his front yard, and there was a visitor. The visitor looked directly at him and said, "I want some beer." And the ECKist realized that he'd left his five liters of beer back at the office.

"If you want the beer, just go to the office and collect it yourself," he told the man in the dream. And just like that, the visitor disappeared.

When the dreamer woke up, this experience was so real to him that he couldn't tell the difference between it and his waking state. And after that dream, his desire for beer began to fall off until he had no

When the dreamer woke up, this experience was so real to him that he couldn't tell the difference between it and his waking state.

The Inner Master helps those people who are ready to drop some habit that's standing in their way on the spiritual path to God.

desire for it again.

This is one of the ways that the Inner Master works. He helps those people who are ready to drop some habit that's standing in their way on the spiritual path to God.

POWERFUL FRIENDS

In ECK, we realize that smoking is also very detrimental. We knew this long before all the current medical studies came out about how primary smoke is very destructive to the health of the smoker and secondary smoke can harm other people in the room with the smoker.

Smoke in an area keeps the Mahanta's presence away.

The Mahanta is always with you, but there are times when a person may block out the presence, help, and protection of the Master because of this addiction to smoking. But the Mahanta stays with these people anyway, in spite of themselves. Because it is very difficult to break habits like drinking and smoking, especially if they've embedded themselves over the years.

A woman had just had her Third Initiation and decided to call her mother. Her mother was in her seventies. She asked her mother if she would like to go out for dinner. They enjoyed each other's company. The mother was delighted to do it.

The mother is not an ECKist, and she is a smoker. They went to a restaurant and had a meal and good conversation. At the end of the meal they were just about ready to go, when the mother sat back in her chair. Now she wanted to smoke; if you're into the smoking habit, it's one of those pleasures after the meal that really adds to the meal. It's hard for nonsmokers to believe.

The mother was digging around in her purse. And her daughter was saying to herself, *It would be very nice if smoke didn't ruin the day of my Third Initiation.* But this was her mother. She loved her. And what could she say?

Her mother was digging around in her purse, looking and looking for her cigarettes. For the first time in nearly sixty years, her mother didn't have her cigarettes with her. The ECKist was just sitting there, grateful and smiling slightly to herself and to the Mahanta.

Her mother caught her smiling and said, "You must have some powerful friends up there." Her mother always had her cigarettes with her.

The daughter said, "Of course I do."

It was one of those bonds of love where the parent accepts the daughter, and the daughter accepts the parent. Each accepts the beliefs and habits of the other person because of the bond of love that's between the two.

Sometimes you find yourself in a situation that's very uncomfortable. And you wonder what to do. A very quick and easy thing to do is to silently say the inner name of the Mahanta: *Wah Z,* or *Z.* Or you can just say Harold. It makes no difference to me. Names come and go. Z is my spiritual name. It goes way back.

A very quick and easy thing to do is to silently say the inner name of the Mahanta: Wah Z, or Z.

NEW NEIGHBORS

An ECK couple had moved into a neighborhood. And their neighbors were new to the neighborhood as well. So they got together to have a nice chat one evening.

And as they were talking, it came out that both women had grown up in very poor families. The

ECKist woman said that her mother had been widowed very early, with young children. But she did whatever she had to, took jobs here and there, and she made a very happy life for her family.

The other woman felt that her mother had neglected her. She had always held it against her mother. Now the mother had become aged. Although the daughter had a loving husband and two lovely children, she really wanted to make her mother feel all the frustration and anger she felt after having been neglected as a child.

The two couples had been trying to have a nice social evening when the second woman began to lose it. She got very emotional about her mother. Her husband was embarrassed, probably thinking to himself, *My wife is talking about all these past hardships in such an undignified way, things that took place years ago. What difference could it make today? She's spoiling the evening with our new neighbors. This is going to be some neighborhood for us!*

The ECKists just sat there. The wife quickly asked inwardly, "Wah Z, what do I do?" And just that quickly, the answer came back to her. "Listen. Just listen."

And so very patiently and quietly, the ECKist and her husband listened to this woman as she began to speak about the anger that had been bottled up inside her for years. Her husband didn't even know that the anger was so deep and so violent. Such a deep angry force was inside his wife, and he had had no idea. The woman had been to doctors, trying to talk it out. But nothing had really done the trick.

When all this anger had boiled out, the woman finally got herself under control. And she apologized. "Thank you for listening," she said. "This is the first time anyone has really ever listened to me."

"Thank you for listening," she said. "This is the first time anyone has really ever listened to me."

She was thirty-eight years old. And this was the first time she felt that anyone had ever listened to her. It's sad that it took thirty-eight years. But on the other hand, it did happen. And it happened because there was an ECKist there, and the Inner Master had said to her, "Listen. Just listen."

So often, we would be better off as vehicles for God—serving life and creation—if we would listen more and give advice less.

The ECKist realized that the other couple was going to have to work through this with the wife's mother in their own way, at their own pace. Eventually it will work out in a way that is in harmony with them. The ECKist did what she could by just listening. But now it is up to the couple to address this problem themselves, in whatever way they can. They will find a way to work out their karma and come into some state of balance that they have not been in before.

WALK WITH ME, MAHANTA

A therapist in Europe has taught the HU—this love song to God—to hundreds of her patients. One of the patients loved the HU, and he would always sing it, but he had this aversion or resistance to Eckankar. They had occasionally talked about Eckankar. He didn't like the resistance, but he couldn't help feeling it.

One day he was talking about it, and the therapist said, "If you want to, why don't you call upon the Inner Master and ask for help so that you can overcome this resistance?"

The patient said he very much wanted to. So the therapist gave him a spiritual exercise where he could invite the Inner Master to help overcome this

> So often, we would be better off as vehicles for God— serving life and creation— if we would listen more and give advice less.

resistance to the teachings of ECK because that's what the man wanted to do. Otherwise she wouldn't have suggested it.

About a week later, the patient came back to the doctor and said, "I have a wonderful story to tell you."

The night after his last treatment, he'd gone home to bed, and he was feeling bad. The flu was coming on, he was in pain, and at the same time, his heart was heavy because the daughter of a dear friend had been in a car accident. She had suffered a fractured skull. The doctors who were treating the accident victim were saying, "It doesn't look good. It doesn't look as if she's going to make it."

That night the man did the spiritual exercise the therapist had given him. He sang HU, and then before he went to sleep, he said, "Mahanta, I don't need help tonight. But could you look in on the daughter of my friend?"

The ECK Masters usually don't do such a thing. There is a spiritual law that says you cannot ask ECK Masters to interfere in other people's lives. The Master is always here, but he probably won't do anything in the way of healing because it's invading another person's state of consciousness to do anything without their permission. And you don't do that.

But the Mahanta did help the man Soul Travel to the hospital. The man found himself at the bedside of the daughter of his friend. He was seated by the bed, with his hand on her head. And as he sat there, he fell asleep.

When he woke up the next morning, his flu symptoms and pain were gone. He felt great.

And a day later, his friend told him, "A miracle happened in the hospital two days ago. My daughter is starting to recover. They didn't think she'd make

There is a spiritual law that says you cannot ask ECK Masters to interfere in other people's lives.

it, but she's going to be fine."

The patient realized something: the moment he had Soul Traveled to the bedside of the injured daughter was when the healing had begun. At exactly that moment, the friend's daughter had begun to recover.

Why could this person Soul Travel to the bedside of the girl and put his hand on her head? Because there was a strong love bond there, and this man had a karmic relationship with that family. And in that situation, he could do something that an ECK Master cannot and would not do. In other words, he could get into the area of someone else's healing without permission.

BLUE STAR PROTECTION

Some people learn about the Blue Star of the Mahanta years before they hear about Eckankar. That's because the presence of the Mahanta has always been here. Sometimes the ECK teachings are out in the forefront of society and then they go into the background again—for decades or even longer. But the teachings of ECK have always been here and will always be here.

In the 1930s during the Depression, times were very hard. There was just no money. In the wintertime, a certain family would rent a place in town. But then in the summer to save rent they would move to a lake where they had a little camp set up. And this is where they lived through the summer because there was no cash.

The father was away building cottages. That was the only work he could get during the Depression. He would come home every few months to visit his family.

Some people learn about the Blue Star of the Mahanta years before they hear about Eckankar.

One summer night, the mother said she had a special treat for the family. "After supper tonight," she told her two daughters, "we're going to a movie in town." Nowadays with cable TV, a movie is no big deal. But it was a big event for this family because their camp at the lake was ten miles outside of town. They hardly ever got into town, so to make the drive to see a movie was really something.

After supper, they all went into town. It was a big event. They were going to see *King Kong*. It's become one of those cult classics. Everybody loves it today. But in the 1930s, the consciousness of people was different, especially in children. Children today see many monster movies, and some of them have bad dreams. But in the 1930s, these types of movies were rare.

One of the little girls was seven or eight at the time. As they went into the theater, she felt very proud to be treated like an adult. Then the movie began. It was pretty good.

But then King Kong began to step on people in cars, and the little girl became very frightened. It scared her right to her heart. And she didn't know what to do.

She leaned over to her mother and said, "I'm going to go out in the lobby for a little while." And the mother just assumed that her daughter was going out to the bathroom. But the daughter never came back. She went out in the lobby, and the sound of King Kong stomping around on people and trashing towns and cities was still going on. It bothered her so much, she went outside. Then she walked away from the theater far enough so that she couldn't hear any sounds from inside the building.

When the movie was over, her mother and sister

came out. The mother was very angry. She had stayed inside and watched the rest of the show; she didn't come looking for her daughter. But she was very angry, and she began to scold her daughter. "Where were you?" she said. "You can't go running off like that."

As they drove the ten miles back out into the country that night, the little girl was still very scared. She kept looking out the window for King Kong, waiting to get crushed by a giant foot. She was terrified.

Her mother put her to bed, and the girl lay in her little camp bed that night in their tent, her eyes shut, trying to go to sleep. And suddenly, she found herself out of the body above their camp. She was on a blue star.

The Blue Star is important because it is the Blue Light of the Mahanta. It is a sign of the Mahanta, the Inner Master. The Blue Star was protection for her back then. As the little girl was up there with the blue star, the star was throwing out golden rays of light all through the campsite, covering the forest along the lake. With these rays of light came an incredible feeling of peace and love. Then the little girl went to sleep, and she was never bothered by that particular fear again.

Years later, she came across the teachings of ECK. She found out about the Blue Star and realized that it was a sign of the divine love that comes from the Holy Spirit.

GIVING A LITTLE EXTRA

A woman worked at the ECK Spiritual Center in Minneapolis, and after a few years she and her husband decided to move to Europe. When they got there, she had a hard time finding work. She didn't

The Blue Star is important because it is the Blue Light of the Mahanta.

know what to do. Three months had passed. And then one day her niece called and said, "I saw an opening at the British Embassy; they're looking for a secretary. Maybe you could apply."

This ECKist has wonderful skills. We missed her when she left, but we were happy that she was going to a new life with her husband.

The day of the interview, the Inner Master told her, "This first interview is going to go OK."

So she got in the car and began driving to the interview. She came to a tollgate on the road and tried to pay the toll. She threw in her money. But the gate didn't lift to let her pass. *Maybe I have to give just a little bit more money,* she thought. She threw a little bit more money in, and the gate still didn't go up. And she was just about ready to back up and go through another gate when an attendant came out and put up the gate so she could drive through. The woman took this as a waking dream.

A waking dream is something that happens in the outer, everyday life that has spiritual significance. The Mahanta was using an incident in her daily life to show her something about the future. In other words, it was the ECK-Vidya.

She realized that whatever was coming, she would have to give just a little bit more—even as she had thrown a few more coins in at the tollbooth. And she also saw how even that extra amount wouldn't be enough. She would need help from another source. When the attendant came out, to her that meant that there would be help from the Inner Master.

The interview went pretty well until she took the typing test. The keyboard in that country had the keys for the punctuation marks in different places than on the American keyboard she was used to. She

A waking dream is something that happens in the outer, everyday life that has spiritual significance.

was trying to pick it up quickly and do a good job, because she had been an excellent typist in the States. But her typing test wasn't as good as it should have been.

She's an excellent worker in so many different ways. Just one of those exceptional people with very good spiritual insight. One of those sweet people about whom you say, "I'm proud to know you." I'm glad such a person is in ECK and that there are many more like her in Eckankar.

The British interviewer was very distant, very cool, and the ECKist thought the interview seemed as if it hadn't gone very well. When she got home, she thought back to the experience with the tollbooth where her coins didn't work the first time.

She said, "I'm going to have to give a little bit more."

So she wrote a little letter to the interviewer at the British Embassy and said, "I didn't do very well on the typing test, but I do have a Norwegian keyboard at home and I will practice. It won't be long before I will be able to type quickly."

A little while later, she got an invitation to come for a second interview. And shortly after that she got word that she had been hired at the British Embassy. She finally had a job. The interviewer wrote her a note. He said, "Just to confirm, you weren't dreaming when you were offered the job," which was funny because so much of what had happened in getting the job had involved waking dreams. She thought it was a very nice touch.

"I NEED SOMETHING TO CONVINCE ME"

Last October, we had the ECK Worldwide Seminar in Atlanta, Georgia. A couple that was new to

Eckankar went to it. They had become members the previous January. The husband was listening to the Friday night talk, and all the stories sounded familiar. His wife wanted to listen to the talk, but her husband kept saying, "Aren't these stories old? Haven't we heard these before somewhere?"

She just said, "No." She wanted to listen to the talk.

But he kept at it. When I began telling the next story, the man said, "Haven't we heard that story before?"

She said, "No!" *What does it take to have a minute of peace to listen to this guy onstage?* she was thinking.

That was Friday night. The same thing happened on Saturday night at the talk. The man began asking his daughter, "You sure we haven't heard these talks before?" He said it was like watching TV reruns in summer. "I've heard everything before. Not exactly like it, but real close," he kept saying.

By the time the seminar was over, the man had pestered not only his wife and his daughter but also their friends, saying, "You're sure he hasn't told that story before?"

His wife began to have experiences in the dream state with the Light and Sound.

"For the last time, no!" his wife told him, because he was starting to get on everybody's nerves. And the man couldn't believe it. Then as they were driving home on Sunday, all of a sudden the wife said, "Hey, you know, two weeks ago you had a dream about that baseball story." And suddenly he remembered. The story wasn't exactly the same as I told at the seminar, but it was very, very close. And the story about the plumber: it was very, very close.

His wife had made contact with the ECK teachings before he had, and she began to have experiences in the dream state with the Light and Sound of God. But she didn't tell him. She didn't tell him for some time. Then finally she told him. And gradually the man began having his own experiences.

This is a truly vital spiritual path. These things happen. These inner experiences happen that give you a vitality and insight into life that you haven't probably had before.

As they were driving home, the man suddenly remembered something else. Not long before, he'd said to his wife, "I need something to convince me." And this experience convinced him that all the stories he heard were indeed in the future. They were already contained there. Whatever the talk material was to be that night, he had already seen it on the Time Track in an inner experience. That's why he had seen and heard all those stories before.

These inner experiences happen that give you a vitality and insight into life that you haven't probably had before.

A Spiritual Door

The man also remembered another experience he'd had in a dream. In the dream was a huge door with the number 127 on it.

When he woke up, he told his wife about it. He said, "I saw this huge door with 127 printed right on it. I wonder what it means." For some reason, his wife began to count off 127 days into the future. It happened to fall right on the weekend of the Atlanta seminar.

The man realized that the Inner Master, the Mahanta, was telling him that a spiritual door would open in his life at that seminar.

When these two experiences had finally sunk in, the man told his wife, "I'm convinced. I'm convinced there's something to these ECK teachings." Some come easy, some come hard. So he was one of those who came hard.

REMEMBER TO ASK, REMEMBER TO LISTEN

It's not to say that the teachings of ECK are easy or that the proof you have today is going to last through tomorrow or the day after. Sometimes the tests of life make it very, very difficult.

You are more alive than you've ever been before.

You wonder sometimes. You may say, "I've made a wrong turn," because often when you first come to a true spiritual path, you find your karma speeds up. You are more alive than you've ever been before. But sometimes you wish you weren't because you're scrambling—you're using every bit of your spiritual creativity to figure out what to do next.

Just remember to sing HU and call upon the Mahanta. Remember to ask, "What do I do now?" and listen. Listen, and listen again. And then wait and watch for the Holy Spirit to open a way for you to go to the next step in your spiritual life.

ECK Springtime Seminar, New York, New York,
Saturday, April 15, 1995

Law number two is: Love is the first and great commandment.

7

FIVE SPIRITUAL LAWS OF THIS WORLD

I'd like to welcome you to the Sunday-morning session of the ECK Springtime Seminar, on Easter morning. A very special day of hope for many people in the Christian world.

I want to cover three areas. First, I'd like to pass on something that may be of help to some of you in matters of health. Second is to talk about five spiritual laws of this world. The third area is more important: a fuller understanding of what consciousness is and how divine love comes through Soul in other forms than just the human form, like animals and so on.

LEARNING ABOUT HEALTH

I've learned a lot about health in this past year. I'm getting stronger. I still have to be very careful, and I'm taking it one seminar at a time.

I don't know how I will feel after a seminar until I let the effects settle in and see how it is. I'm much stronger than I was at the 1994 ECK Worldwide Seminar in Atlanta, but there's a long way to go. I'm getting a lot of rest and have more strength and more energy. I'm also getting help from some very good people in alternative medicine.

These health conditions are part of the human condition. They're part of the spiritual path. They're part of this world.

My first problem was with electromagnetic radiation. It looked like this was the primary cause of things not working correctly. When I finally said, "OK, I've got a problem. I have to put my attention on healing," I found that the veils went back and back. As you work back, you discover even more primary causes.

There has to be a total healing working all the way back.

One of the new members in ECK from Minnesota was kind enough to send me a book that has some very good information in it. It would be good to keep in your first-aid kit just as a source of hope.

I can't guarantee that its information is 100 percent accurate because this is earth. Nothing is perfect, no matter how good your source of information. There will always be someone to do a study to show that something doesn't work. Others will do a study to show that it's working very well.

We're all unique individuals. We've all grown up under different conditions, and today we all live under different conditions. And we bring our strengths and weaknesses with us, through our genes.

We're all unique individuals.

A HELPFUL BOOK

This book is called *The Cure for All Cancers* by Dr. Hulda Clark. It's from ProMotion Publishing out of San Diego, California. I don't have any financial connection with these books that I mention. It's just something worthwhile. It's worth a look, something for the first-aid kit. This researcher has done some very interesting work. Cancer patients came to her after the medical doctors had no hope for them. She would take the very worst cases and try to help them. And she's been able to help some people.

This doctor found a very curious connection that I haven't seen anywhere before. First she noticed that all of the cancer patients that came to her also had flukes, a kind of parasite. And second, she found propyl alcohol in the body at the same time.

Propyl alcohol—like isopropyl alcohol, rubbing alcohol—is in cosmetics. It's in a lot of different products. And some people, because of their environmental sensitivities, are not able to handle this combination. All of her patients had both elements in their systems, which may or may not be the reason for their cancer.

She has an entire cleansing program to first get rid of the propyl alcohol in the system, then the parasites. Step-by-step, she shows a person who is in very serious trouble and has no more hope from the medical profession what to do to regain health. Whether or not this works in all conditions, I would rather doubt.

HANDLING TOXINS

Someone raised a very interesting point. He said, "I don't think the title is correct." Nor do I. What about people who are caught in a nuclear disaster, such as at Chernobyl?

It seems to me that there are two ways that people can overload on toxins. One is the slow, natural way of everyday living—getting too many pesticides in their food, perhaps a weak genetic structure, or electromagnetic radiation. This builds up something

I would call organic overload. It takes place over time.

A catastrophic event such as Chernobyl, where the body is hit by enormous amounts of radiation, overloads all the organs at once. In most cases, it's difficult to reverse something like that.

I'm mentioning this book as something that came across my desk. There's some very interesting information in there for people who have gone the route with the medical profession, received no help, and have been given up for lost. It's something to look into. I'm making no guarantees about it because I am not licensed to do such a thing. And if I were, I suppose I would have my share of failures in that field. Any field of medicine has its failures as well as its successes.

I mention books like this one when there is good material I think would benefit your spiritual well-being. I just bring it to your attention. Then you can look further into it if you wish to.

These five laws are important when looking at the political and religious fields.

FIVE SPIRITUAL LAWS

I want to mention five spiritual laws of this world. I'm not saying "*the* five," as if that's all there are. These five laws are important laws, especially when you're looking at the political and religious fields today.

Many of our spiritual leaders are having a problem trying to figure out which way's up and which way's down. We're at a critical point again, not just in the United States, but in many countries of the world. There's a cash-flow crisis. There isn't enough cash to go around because of the enormous debt burdens on a number of different societies. This causes a problem in day-to-day living for a lot of people. It's already been a problem since the early 1990s. It just depends upon which part of the world you're in and where the hot spot is at that particular time.

Beginning of Human Life

The first law deals with the beginning of human life. And the beginning of human life is when breath comes into the fetus.

Readers Digest had an article about sextuplets, six little babies, and how they were born and survived. Wonderful story. Such medical wonders are available to us today. And yet our legislators are always trying to figure out how can they make a law more specific—thinking that in making the law more specific, it's going to answer any question in the best way possible. But in becoming too specific, they complicate the problem because exceptions come up. They have to make laws to deal with those exceptions, and these laws breed other exceptions. And they have to make new laws to take care of those exceptions.

If these people would work from an overview and understand that the answers are in their own Christian Bibles, they would have a little bit more peace. They would let life move along more peacefully for the rest of us.

Leaders are supposed to be more knowledgeable. But sometimes they're just more powerful.

They have more of a lust for power and control than the average person. That's why they're in those positions, not necessarily because they have great ability to lead, not because they know more about people or conditions.

So law number one: The beginning of human life is when breath comes into the fetus.

The first law deals with the beginning of human life.

The beginning of human life is when breath comes into the fetus.

The backup for this in the Christian Bible is Genesis 2:7. "And the Lord God formed man of the dust of the ground and breathed into his nostrils the breath of life; and man became a living soul." The key point is "and breathed into his nostrils the breath of life." I won't go into that any further because we've beat that into the ground over the past few years. It's an emotional issue. You're not going to win on it.

LOVE COMES FIRST

Law number two is: Love is the first and great commandment.

If the leaders in a society would understand this law, I think we would have better leadership. And I think there would be better people in the country who would work under these leaders if the people understood this too.

This law can also be called the rule of spiritual law. In Matthew 22:37–39, Jesus said, "Thou shalt love the Lord thy God with all thy heart, and with all thy soul, and with all thy mind. This is the first and great commandment. And the second is like unto it, Thou shalt love thy neighbour as thyself."

If the leaders and the people in a society would take these two laws to heart, this would be an entirely different place. But most of the time, we find that the human condition is self-serving, selfish. It wants power and control rather than to serve God and life with love. And this is the great problem.

OUR PERSONAL RESPONSIBILITY

The third law deals with the welfare system. It tells about the responsibility we have to make our own way as much as we can in this world.

I'm not talking about people who receive retirement benefits, because they've paid into a system. According to the laws of society, they have a right to retire. Because when you get older, you simply don't have the physical energy of a young person to earn a good living. It's not possible.

Law number three is: Work for your food.

This comes from Paul in his second letter to the Thessalonians. I am quoting from the King James Version, but its language is sometimes a little obscure. I grew up with it, and I was very used to it, so it's easy for me. But some of you wouldn't have a chance—especially if you don't have a Christian background—with the King James Version of the Bible. I'll give you an example: "Withdraw yourself from every brother that walketh disorderly, and not after the tradition which he received of us." Paul is saying: Don't associate with people who are disorderly because they are not following in the tradition that Paul and the Apostles were trying to give to the early Christians.

Today we in ECK are in the same position of trying to set an example for those who are going to come after us. And it's very difficult.

Paul goes on, "For yourselves know how ye ought to follow us: for we behaved not ourselves disorderly among you." He was saying, We were decent people when we were with you. We respected you.

> *Law number three is: Work for your food.*

LIVING A LIFE OF LOVE

"Neither did we eat any man's bread for nought" means that we didn't just take somebody else's bread without doing something in return. "But wrought with labour and travail night and day." We worked and did whatever we could, we did whatever our mission was. Maybe they were missionaries and maybe that was the work that they did to earn their food. Or maybe they washed pots and pans for the family. Maybe they carried wood. But they did all this work night and day "that we might not be chargeable to any of you." Which basically means that we didn't owe you anything in the way of rent or anything else. Nobody could say, "You didn't carry your own weight." Paul was saying, We carried our own weight, and this is the tradition that we were trying to give to the rest of you. These are good principles.

And we're addressing the welfare system. Paul continues, "Not because we have not power, but to make ourselves an ensample unto you to follow us." In other words, he was saying, We could be the big guys and say, "We're in town. Take care of us. We're going to do our preaching. Feed us; give us room and board." We could have pulled rank on you, and you would have to put up with it. But we didn't do that. We wanted to be an example for you.

Then he says, "For even when we were with you, this we commanded you." And this is the important point. The people who are putting together legislation for the reform of the welfare system need to understand this: "That if any would not work, neither should he eat." Very simple, very straightforward.

And then he closes: "For we hear that there are some which walk among you disorderly, working not at all, but are busybodies" (2 Thessalonians 3:6–11). Very nice touch.

Law number four deals with our duty to the government regarding tax levies. Give tribute to God and Caesar.

OUR DUTY TO THE GOVERNMENT

Law number four deals with our duty to the government regarding tax levies. Law number four: Give tribute to God and Caesar.

The Pharisees were trying to trick Jesus into making statements against the Roman government. If they could do this, they could bring the Roman government down on him and have him put in jail. So someone asked him, "Is it lawful to give tribute unto Caesar, or not?"

Jesus was very sharp. "Show me a coin."

They said, "Sure."

They gave him a coin, worth maybe twenty cents. "Whose image is on this coin?" he said.

They said, "Caesar's."

And Jesus said, "Render," which means give, "Render therefore unto Caesar the things which are Caesar's; and unto God the things that are God's" (Matthew 22:17, 21). And they marveled at how he had sidestepped their trap.

GOVERNMENT'S DUTY TO THE PEOPLE

Law number four was about the people's duty to the government. Law number five is about the government's duty to the people.

This is the one that government officials like to forget about. When they forget about it and take more than their due through taxes, they enslave the people they are ruling. If you don't have money in a society, you have no freedom. The government leaders are all too human, working and wrestling with the karmic problems of control and power. Don't expect them to be working in your best interest. They're not. They're working in their own best interest.

This is not an indictment against any political party. Ninety-five percent of the people who work in politics have already prostituted themselves just by the mere fact of being there. Because it often shows an abnormal desire for power.

Law number five is about the government's duty to the people.

Law number
five: Reward
the laborer.

Law number five: Reward the laborer.

In 1 Timothy 5:18, Paul says, "Thou shalt not muzzle the ox that treadeth out the corn. And, The labourer is worthy of his reward."

Paul tried to explain the same concept to the Corinthians in another letter. And he quotes this law again, "Thou shalt not muzzle the mouth of the ox that treadeth out the corn." Does God take care of oxen? he asked them. Well, from his viewpoint, no. God takes care of people, not oxen. So he continues his argument, "Or saith he it altogether for our sakes?" And then he answers himself, "For our sakes, no doubt, this is written."

Here's the whole purpose of incentive, of why people work: "that he that ploweth should plow in hope; and that he that thresheth in hope should be partaker of his hope" (1 Corinthians 9:9–10). If you're plowing and somebody demands that you give your entire crop to Caesar, there's no incentive for you to work. That's what they used to do in the Soviet Union. People didn't work, and today there is no Soviet Union. It was a government trying to enslave its people.

The government said, "Don't worry about things. We'll take care of you." And all they did was suppress and make slaves of their people.

Socialism is the same as communism, just not quite as strong—yet. We have to look out for the spiritual freedom involved in these laws that are reflected in the Christian Bible.

Whenever I talk like this, I usually come out the loser on both ends. ECKists are upset because I talked about the Christian Bible and these laws. And people who are not in ECKANKAR are upset at me because I dare to interpret the Christian Bible. Well, I've studied it a long time.

There are some good things in all the different scriptures. We try not to be exclusive and say that the ECK scriptures are the final word because there are wonderful things in the Christian scriptures. But I feel the teachings of ECK go further in the demonstration of how to live a life of love instead of law.

LEARN TO LOVE YOURSELF

I would like to go on to something which I feel is higher and more spiritual. And this is how the love of the Holy Spirit works through higher law than human law. This probably demonstrates law number two more closely, which is love. Love God first, and then love your neighbor as yourself.

You cannot love your neighbor unless you first love yourself. This is very important.

Love your neighbor as yourself doesn't mean a lot more than yourself. It means you have to love yourself first. And with all the guilt that is sometimes loaded on people in Christianity, I wonder how anybody can love himself or herself. That's the paradox and the dilemma in Christianity. There's so much guilt loaded upon people that they cannot love themselves.

Love yourself first. That means you have to have a good opinion of yourself as a spiritual being.

CHILD OF GOD

After all, you are a child of God. Why not have a good, healthy opinion about yourself? You are worth something. The basic principle of ECK is: Soul exists because God loves It. You exist because God loves you, and that's all the reason there needs to be. You are important because you exist.

This is sometimes the starting point. Once you reach that point, you can say, "I'm worth something

Love God first, and then love your neighbor as yourself.

Love yourself first. That means you have to have a good opinion of yourself as a spiritual being.

because God loves me. I am Soul."

And if you can carry this with you, then you can go out into the world and love your neighbor as yourself. Then, but not before. And if you can do this truly from your heart, this will be an entirely different world.

But since it's not an entirely different world, I would have to guess that many of the major religions have failed in their message. Maybe they're doing the best they can in this theater of the human condition where people are learning to overcome their passions so that they can rise to a higher state of consciousness through their own experiences in life.

You learn that you are totally responsible for everything that you do.

EVERYTHING COMES BACK TO YOU

You break the laws, and you pay for breaking the laws. You let your anger go wild, and it comes back to you at work and in your family. You speed in traffic, and a police officer pulls you over.

These are the causes and effects that occur in life, and each time, you learn something. You may learn the wrong thing, but eventually these things add up. And you learn that you are totally responsible for everything that you do. And that everything that comes into your life has come back to you.

This is a hard lesson for people because it totally wipes out the victim consciousness.

The big escape clause today is, "I will sue. I will get rich." It's trying to get something for nothing. People want to believe somebody else is responsible, but it's a lie. It's a lie of the negative power, the Kal force. And when people fall for this lie, they're not falling into riches. They're falling deeper into spiritual slavery. And these people will try to pull others down with them into lower states.

And that's OK. Because a lot of people belong there. It's part of this path to God. It's part of Soul's progression from the lower states to the higher states.

Examples of Pure Love

One of the radio commentators I sometimes listen to is into politics. He has this funny view of animals. He thinks that since animals can't discuss politics intelligently, they must be a lower form of life. I think animals know there is no sense in discussing politics in the first place. And this qualifies them to be a higher life-form. But I would make some people very angry if they heard me say this.

People have such a high opinion of themselves—in the wrong way. This is vanity, which goes along with power and control. A lot of people in the public eye are working with these negative habits of power, control, and vanity. Vanity's a good one, because it makes them feel so good, so powerful, and so right. They want to make other people do things their way. That's where the problem comes in.

If you're writing for film or television, the directive is always "Show, don't tell." But people are always talking. They talk about love, but they show something entirely different. Animals can't talk. So they show. That's why they're so effective—what you see is what you get.

Animals sometimes have this capacity to transfer God's love directly to the ones they love in such a simple and clear way. I'm talking about those animals who are in the higher states.

If the cat likes you, it walks up to you and purrs. If it doesn't like you for whatever reason—it doesn't. That's how it is. The human's the loser as far as the cat's concerned. The cat doesn't care.

Animals sometimes have this capacity to transfer God's love directly to the ones they love in such a simple and clear way.

Animals are often examples to people about how to live the spiritual laws.

Dogs care. The wonderful thing about dogs is their loyalty to their masters. It's a total, pure love. If you ever want to find an example of loyalty and love to live a better Christian life or a better life as an ECKist, just look at how dogs love their owners. They just love. It's incredible. The owners may mistreat them but these animals just love them anyway. And they love with such a pure love; it's just beautiful.

Animals are often examples to people about how to live the spiritual laws.

A BOND OF LOVE

A thirteen-year-old girl moved to a new town with her family, and she was lonesome. One day, she was with her mother, sitting in front of a store on some bags of fertilizer. The father was inside the store paying for supplies. As the mother and daughter were sitting there, all of a sudden they saw something moving behind the bags of fertilizer.

A little black-and-white kitten came out. It seemed lost, so the thirteen-year-old girl put it inside her shirt and carried it home. When they got home, the girl showed the cat to Dad. He wasn't real happy, but he said, "All right, you can keep it."

This cat was a companion for this young girl for almost twenty years. They were together until she turned thirty-two. And at that time, it was getting near to the end of the cat's life.

They had been great companions. The woman had found that the longer they were together, the more she loved the cat. Her love for the cat grew deeper and deeper. And about that time, she read one of the stories in the *ECKANKAR Journal* that told of a cat owner whose cat had reincarnated to be back with her. So the woman often told her cat, "Tiger Lily, if you ever want to come back, please come back. Because I love you."

Finally it was time for Tiger Lily to go. She had spent many good years of happiness, love, and service on this earth.

For two and a half years after the cat translated, this woman wondered, *If Tiger Lily ever comes back, I wonder how I will recognize her.* So she tried to think of some symbols, something that might work, something out of the ECK teachings. How would she be able to recognize her dear friend Tiger Lily?

About this time she got married to a wonderful man. And this man had a wonderful dog. Unfortunately, the dog liked to chase cats. Now the woman worried that if Tiger Lily ever came back, how would things work out?

One night she had a dream, and in the dream she suddenly knew that Tiger Lily was back. When she woke up, she said, "I know Tiger Lily's back now. I'd better talk to the dog and see what the dog feels about this. How would the dog like a cat here?"

So she said to the dog, "How would you like a cat?" Remember, this dog likes to chase cats. He wagged his tail. Of course she took it as a good sign.

The dog probably took it as a good sign too.

CAT COMES BACK

After her dream, she sometimes saw people giving away kittens. Each time she said, "How am I going to know? Is that the kitten? Is that Tiger Lily?" But she finally gave up and said to the Mahanta, "I don't think I'll be able to figure this out with my head. I'm just going to have to trust my heart."

One day, she was over at her husband's parents'

"I don't think I'll be able to figure this out with my head. I'm just going to have to trust my heart."

place, and they had just had dinner. The couple was ready to leave when a young kitten came running down the street.

Cats are very nonchalant about things like reincarnation. "There's my owner," the cat probably said as she came running up to the woman. "I've been waiting for you." This woman looked at the kitten. It didn't look like her other kitten, but she picked it up.

The kitten immediately licked her on the nose and began purring. And the woman's head was spinning. Things were going too fast; she couldn't figure this out. She had waited two and a half years. She had wondered, *How will I know? I don't want to get the wrong cat. I want to get Tiger Lily.* And here was this kitten, just so glad to see her, licking her nose and purring.

Her mother-in-law said, "I know where that cat belongs. It lives down the street. We'll go ask the family if you can have it."

"No, no," the woman stammered. "I don't know, I really don't think . . . "

But the mother-in-law said, "Come on. We'll go over there." So she dragged this woman over to the neighbors. "Go on and ask them," she said.

The woman still couldn't talk. She was stammering, unable to get any words out.

Her mother-in-law said, "Could she have this kitten?"

The neighbors said, "Sure. And if it doesn't work out, just bring the kitten back."

So the woman got her cat back. There were problems at first. The dog did like to chase the cat, so they had to work with the dog. And the kitten hadn't been completely house trained, so there were messes on the rugs. They had to deal with that. But each time the ECKist looked into the cat's eyes, she could see it was Tiger Lily. There was no question.

Those of you who've had a pet that's come back—as I have, many times—know about this.

One of my cat friends was named Tiger. Cats didn't live long on the farm, maybe eight, nine, ten years, because life was hard. But Tiger would always come back. She was such a loving cat, very affectionate, like Tiger Lily in this story.

Once the owner looked in her cat's eyes, she knew: here was her old friend come back.

Once the owner looked in her cat's eyes, she knew: here was her old friend come back. This is something we can accept very easily in ECK, because we know. We know about such things. Our teaching accepts reincarnation. Christianity doesn't, and that's why some Christians have such a very hard time with this concept. And that's why many of you who were Christians have come to Eckankar. You knew there was more to life than just the values of the human consciousness.

A HOME FOR C. J.

A woman and her husband were moving from the U.S. to another country, and they had to find a home for their two cats. One was Sam; the other was C. J. Sam could go with the woman's parents, because Sam was a nice, affectionate cat. But the family couldn't take more than Sam because they already had one cat. Two cats was OK. Three cats would be too many. So the couple had to find a home for C. J.

C. J. was a nice cat as long as he wasn't kept indoors. He liked freedom.

The woman did everything she could to find a good home for C. J. She left little ads at pet stores, at grocery stores, on bulletin boards. She ran ads in newspapers. She did everything. One day a woman saw the ad and took C. J. home. Two days later she brought him back. The cat had hissed and growled the entire two days. The woman didn't want any part of that.

The time was getting closer for this couple to leave the United States, but they still had this problem with the cat. What would they do with C. J.? It looked like it was going to be the Humane Society and the end of C.J. There was nothing else to do. The ECKist didn't just want to turn him loose outside.

It came right down to the day they were leaving, half an hour before they were to leave. The woman had wanted to clean the carpet in the apartment, but she'd forgotten. As she was out and about doing last-minute errands, she saw a Servicemaster truck. It's from a carpet-cleaning company, she realized.

At this point, she turned it over to the Inner Master and said, "Let thy will be done," to the Holy Spirit.

"If the Mahanta cares enough to remind me to have the carpet cleaned when I've forgotten, maybe the Master will help C. J. find a home," the woman said.

At this point, she turned it over to the Inner Master and said, "Let thy will be done," to the Holy Spirit. "Let thy will be done, not mine anymore, because there's only half an hour left, and I've done the best I could," she said.

Eleventh Hour

She was standing in the apartment, looking at the carpet at the bottom of the stairs that went down into the basement. She had only half an hour left, but instead of leaving early, she decided to replace a little worn piece of carpet. She'd wanted to do it for a while, and she's very handy. She got out her cutting tools, got a new piece of carpet, cut it, and was putting it in. Five minutes before she was planning to walk out the door to leave Minneapolis for good, the phone rang. It was a woman who lived on six acres out in the country, a small farm with miniature goats.

"What about this cat?" the woman asked. "Is it an outdoor cat?"

My goodness, the ECKist thought. She couldn't believe the timing. "Outdoor cat?" she said, "Oh yeah, C. J.'s an outdoor cat, all right."

Then the woman said, "Well, is he a mouser?"

"A mouser? Oh yes." This was starting to sound better and better.

The woman explained, "We've got six acres. We've got these other animals around. We've got children. Lots of space. But we need a mouser because we're starting to get mice."

It sounded perfect. The ECKist arranged to meet the woman halfway—there wasn't much time—since the woman had to come into town for errands. When they met, C. J. jumped right into the woman's car, as if to say, "Let's go." He looked very happy about the whole thing.

On their way out of the U.S., the ECKist called the woman. "How's it going with C. J.?" she asked.

And the woman on the other end of the phone said, "Great. The first night C. J. caught a mouse, and right after that he made friends with the dog. The kids love him. It's working out very well."

Right up to the eleventh hour, the woman didn't know if there was going to be a home for her cat. But she tried to do the best thing up to the very end.

These stories show the love between people and animals, but in many cases they also show the intervention of Divine Spirit through the Mahanta, the

These stories show the love between people and animals, but in many cases they also show the intervention of Divine Spirit through the Mahanta, the Inner Master.

Inner Master. I'm grateful to all of you who tell me these stories. I just pass them along. They're not my stories. They're your stories. They're telling what you have found through your life in ECK.

Spot, the Butterfly

A family was moving from the East Coast of the U.S. out to the West Coast. And as soon as they got there, the mother knew that this was the wrong move. It was a very unfriendly company for her husband, number one. Plus, everything else was just wrong. She was unhappy and fell into depression.

This went on for some time. And then one evening just before dinner, her daughter came in, and on a little piece of paper, she had a butterfly. It was sort of a brown butterfly with dark spots on its wings. It's called a wood nymph.

"Mommy, look what I found outside," the daughter said.

It was getting dark. The mother said, "Before dark, you ought to put the butterfly back outside," because this butterfly was just about at the end of its lifespan.

So the little girl very carefully put the butterfly back on a piece of paper and carried it outside where it was in view from the kitchen window. Later when the little girl had gone to bed, the mother looked out. *Maybe I ought to bring it inside,* the woman thought. *That butterfly isn't going to live long, but it shouldn't have to be out there in the cold. It could be here in the kitchen by the stove where it's warm.*

She went out and brought it in. And this little butterfly then transformed this woman over the next

This little butterfly then transformed this woman over the next three weeks.

three weeks—because that's how long the butterfly lived. It transformed her from a person who was depressed and sad. It began to open and awaken the love within the woman again.

The next morning, the little butterfly was still alive. "Brave little thing," the woman said. "It just seems to sit there. It will probably die pretty soon."

By that afternoon, the woman said, "Maybe there's something I can do for it. Maybe it's hungry. What do you feed a butterfly?" She didn't know. She thought she'd try putting a little bit of honey on her finger. She diluted a drop of honey with water, and she held it down by the butterfly's mouth. The little butterfly's tongue came out, and the butterfly ate the honey.

The next day when the woman tried to feed the butterfly, it had more strength. It came toward her.

Pretty soon the little butterfly didn't want to get off the woman's hand when feeding time was over. It would stay for a while because it began to love her. And she began to love this little butterfly.

One day, she was wearing a woolen garment, and the little butterfly got one of its legs caught in the wool. The leg got pulled off. Now it had only five legs. The woman was horrified. "Oh no, what have I done?"

Even with five legs, the little butterfly would always come out to meet her as much as it could.

As the butterfly neared the end of its three-week visit, the woman felt very bad. One night it looked like it was ready to go. Its wings were quivering, so the woman stayed with the butterfly for a long time. Then finally she said good-bye to it and went to bed.

Next morning when she got up, the butterfly was still alive. So she sang HU. She put the butterfly on her finger and sang HU very gently. And shortly after, the butterfly left.

She put the butterfly on her finger and sang HU very gently.

HELP FROM OTHER SOULS

Sometimes
the Holy Spirit
sends other
Souls to
minister to
people.

In three weeks, this little being had transformed the woman and her entire family. The joy that this butterfly brought into the home was infectious. It caught her husband and her daughter, and especially it caught the woman herself. And the butterfly had taught her some lessons. One, it had taught her patience. And number two, endurance without complaining. Three, it showed her a strong desire to live. And four, it showed her how to love.

This story shows how sometimes the Holy Spirit sends other Souls to minister to people.

Whether or not your philosophy or religion accepts Souls in forms other than the human is unimportant. But if you can accept reincarnation and the fact that Soul takes on many different bodies — and some of these are higher forms than some of the people who are living in human forms — you will find much more joy and happiness in your own life. You'll also find greater understanding of God's true creation. This is truth. It's reality.

A GIFT OF LOVE

A woman had been working for many years. But she came to the point in her life where she had to go through a number of surgeries. Because of the surgeries, she had to quit work. And when she quit work, her source of income dried up. She'd been a postal worker, so she got a pension from the post office. But she and her husband were not able to live at the same level they had before.

To make it worse, with less money, her husband began to scold her constantly. She was sick. She had just come through several operations. She couldn't take care of him as she had before — serve him hand

and foot—and he was complaining all the time. "Why don't you do this for me anymore?" he'd ask.

What the woman missed most of all was being able to take care of her grandson. She loved the little fellow, but she was too weak from the surgeries and couldn't take care of him.

The woman grew more and more depressed. It got so bad that when someone would come up to her, she'd begin to cry. Right out of the blue, she'd begin to cry. And she didn't know what to do about it.

One day, she went to visit her neighbor. The young woman was a licensed daycare person. And she had these tiny two-year-olds. The woman walked up to the gate, and her neighbor came to the gate to let her in. All the little people came up to her, and they said, "Hello."

The woman began to cry, because for the first time she realized one of the main reasons for her depression—she missed her grandson so. The shock from the surgeries and the poisons in her system were certainly contributing to her depression. But what would have helped her most of all would be just to have seen her grandson. And here were all these friendly little people.

And then, a very unusual thing happened. The neighbor kept a cage in the front yard with a beautiful, large, white cockatiel. The neighbor went over to the cage and took the cockatiel out. The woman was standing very close to the bird. And the cockatiel leaned over and kissed her on the cheek.

"I've never seen him do that to anyone before," the neighbor said, very surprised.

And in the next moment, something even more unusual happened. The bird was on a perch next to the woman. And it put out its wing and wrapped it

Soul in a
cockatiel's body
was answering
a call from the
Holy Spirit
which was
saying, "Here's
a fellow Soul
that needs your
love and
comfort."

around her shoulder. The neighbor said, "Look at that. This bird has never kissed anybody on the cheek before, and it's certainly never put its wing around anybody's shoulder."

It was the Holy Spirit's way of bringing love to this woman who couldn't find it at home. Soul in a cockatiel's body was answering a call from the Holy Spirit which was saying, "Here's a fellow Soul that needs your love and comfort."

This is how the Holy Spirit passes comfort to Its creation. It gives love.

Sometimes it's love from other people, people who just listen. But in this woman's case, there was nobody to listen, just people to scold. Except for the bird. The bird was a clear instrument for the Holy Spirit to convey divine love to this woman who had had her share of hardships.

And when this happened, her spirits lightened. And she realized two things. First of all, the Master cared for her. This is how she sees life — the Mahanta is an expression of the divine ECK, the Holy Spirit, in a form that people can understand. And then the woman realized how much she missed her grandson. She realized that this was the real reason for her depression.

At the same time, she saw that she was not alone. This bird putting its wing around her shoulder was the assurance from the Master and from the Holy Spirit that divine love and protection were always with her. The Master was with her, and she was not alone.

And neither are you. Because on your journey home, I am always with you.

ECK Springtime Seminar, New York, New York,
Sunday, April 16, 1995

The Inner Master said to her, "Open your wings, and you will know who you are."

8

OPEN YOUR WINGS

I'm glad so many of you were able to come to this ECK seminar. We'll try to give you something that you can carry with you for more than a few weeks — perhaps your whole lifetime.

TOUCHED BY DIVINE SPIRIT

Every time I give a talk I wonder, *What is there to say? What can help you spiritually in some way?* Most of the help comes inwardly. But those of you who have been members of Eckankar for some time realize that there is another factor working during these talks, and this is the inner connection that you have with Divine Spirit.

It will touch you in some way, in some unexpected way. It will lift you spiritually. I've seen people cry unexpectedly for joy.

These influences from Divine Spirit affect people in ways that surprise even them. I just watch this and try to give you whatever I can as a clear channel for the ECK, the Holy Spirit.

Divine Spirit will touch you in some way, in some unexpected way. It will lift you spiritually.

CHECKING THE STORY

At one ECK seminar I told a story from an ECKist, and it is in chapter 9 of *The Slow Burning Love of God,* Mahanta Transcripts, Book 13. He had told a story of seeing the blue light at his ophthalmologist's office. Afterward, he wrote me. He said that he's always enjoyed my stories but he figured I embellished them. "I'm going to go back and check my journal to see how close your story is to what I told you," he said.

Sometimes when people tell me a story, the ECK opens up and shows me the rest of the story.

He later told me that all the details matched, which was quite a surprise to me. Sometimes when people tell me a story, the ECK opens up and shows me the rest of the story. Then I give this too. People are surprised at this.

One time an ECKist gave me a story that had happened to his father. When I told the story, I added a detail that he hadn't told me. I said, "And Rebazar Tarzs was the person." Rebazar Tarzs is an ECK Master who helps people. Rebazar Tarzs was one of the people who came and helped his father. Later, this ECKist described Rebazar to his father. His father said, "Yes, as a matter of fact there was this man here, and he did look like that. But I don't think I told you about him." I see the rest of the story, and I report it as I see it. I try to be accurate.

SEEING THE INNER SHARIYAT

A woman lives in New Zealand. She's out in the country so she feels isolated from other ECKists. But as a member of Eckankar, she gets the ECK discourses — monthly letters that I send from the ECK Spiritual Center to the members of Eckankar depending upon their level of study. The woman gets this discourse each month, and with the discourse she feels she's part of the body of ECK. She feels this connection with all the other members in Eckankar even though she can't get to town to physically meet with other ECKists.

When she was eleven years old, she was in her bedroom when suddenly one night a green light began to shine in the corner of her room. In the middle of this light she saw a scroll. The light seemed to come from this scroll. She saw characters — letters — written on this scroll. The little girl just looked at it, wondering what this was all about.

In the middle of this light she saw a scroll. The light seemed to come from this scroll.

Then as she watched, the greenish glow and the scroll just faded away. She didn't yet realize that it was the Holy Spirit, the ECK; but she did know that something was leading her on a mystic path with very interesting experiences.

Years later she came in touch with Eckankar. She's seen Rebazar Tarzs and some of the other ECK Masters.

One day she was reading in her ECK discourse that sometimes *The Shariyat-Ki-Sugmad* is seen as a scroll. *The Shariyat-Ki-Sugmad* is the ECK bible. It means Way of the Eternal. As the woman read this, she suddenly remembered her experience as a child and began to get an understanding of what had happened to her way back then. She realized that as a child of eleven she had already had a look at one of the volumes of this holy book, *The Shariyat-Ki-Sugmad*.

There are two volumes out here, and there are twelve volumes on the inner planes. She was able to see one. But she wondered, *What is this? What is happening to me?* And so she eventually found Eckankar.

INNER AND OUTER MASTER

One morning she was doing her contemplation, and the Inner Master came to her. In Eckankar there are two sides to the teaching: the inner and the outer. The outer teachings come from the outer person—myself. I write discourses, I write articles, and I give talks. On the inner side—the greater side—there's a counterpart of myself working with people in the dream state. And here I work with people as the Dream Master.

When people do their spiritual exercises or go into contemplation, in one way or another this inner part of myself—which is a manifestation of Divine Spirit at a certain level—comes and speaks to them or shows them something that is important for their spiritual unfoldment at that moment.

This may sound very far-out for those of you who are new to Eckankar. My apologies, but I sometimes feel an urgency about saying these things.

I work with people as the Dream Master.

STRAIGHT TRUTH

Over the past year I've been very ill. I'm slowly regaining my health and still have a long ways to go. But since this happened, I have this urgency to say what has to be said and let the chips fall where they may. People can believe it, or they can ignore it. They can laugh. They can do what they want. But my job is to tell people about the inner and the outer teachings of ECK.

Those of you who are ready will understand what I'm talking about. And the rest of you who aren't ready won't understand what I'm talking about whether I try to polish it up for you or not. It isn't going to make a bit of difference.

"Send Me a Guardian Angel"

An ECKist lives in New York City with his family. And he's very concerned about living there because of the street crime and the drug problem; there are bad things going on in the streets close by.

His mother is a Catholic. She doesn't know too much about Eckankar. She isn't all that interested.

But he was concerned about her and the rest of the family. So he talked to the inner side, the Mahanta. We say the Mahanta, the Living ECK Master—but the Inner Master or the Dream Master are other terms. He was saying, "If it's OK and if I'm not interfering in my mother's personal space or anything like this, is there some way there can be some protection for her?"

He didn't know that at about the same time he was talking with the Inner Master, his mother was at home praying. She's also very afraid of the crime. So she asked God, "God, please send me a guardian angel."

A short time after that, she was in her living room, and she saw a blue light. The blue light is one of the ways that the Inner Master shows up and marks the presence of safety, protection, or wisdom. And that night as the mother went to sleep—and remember, she knows very, very little about Eckankar—she had a dream. In the dream she had this experience where she said, "I have to sing HU."

HU is the love song to God that we sing. And it's to open your heart—like opening your wings. Opening your wings simply means opening your state of consciousness.

The mother saw a bright light around her, the same kind of bright light that she had seen in her living room. When she mentioned this to her son, he

So she asked God, "God, please send me a guardian angel."

HU is the love song to God that we sing.

told her about the connection between the light and the Inner Master, Wah Z. This Inner Master—the Dream Master—is known as Wah Z. That's the full name. Sometimes for short, Z.

OPEN YOUR WINGS

When the woman in New Zealand was in the middle of contemplation one day, the Inner Master came to her and said, "Open your wings, and you will know who you are." This is the whole point of the path of ECK and these teachings. Open your wings means simply to open your state of consciousness, and then you will know who and what you are.

The Inner Master said to her, "Open your wings, and you will know who you are."

Most people are in the human state of consciousness. This means fears and worries like Am I going to be safe going home? Am I going to be able to pay my rent or mortgage? That's part of the human consciousness—all the circumstances that drive us in our daily life. It's the reason we get a job—so we can survive in a place of our own choosing and care for those who depend on us.

The Inner Master said to her, "Open your wings, and you will know who you are." These talks, inwardly and outwardly, are to help you open your wings.

This means to open your state of consciousness so you can go beyond the human state into one of the higher states of spiritual consciousness.

BEYOND EXPERIENCES

I'm giving you stories of different people's experiences. Ours is a path of experience. Don't believe something because I said it or some other member of ECK said it.

Prove it to yourself. If it works, take it a step further. And if it doesn't work, let it go.

Beyond experience is something much more important, and this is simply learning how to give and receive God's love. And that's not experience. That's a condition. That's being able to open your heart, to open your wings, to accept the gifts of life.

The gifts are all around you all the time. Most often they come to us as acts of kindness by people near us.

The gifts of God come to us most often through other people.

But if we are in the human consciousness, we are sometimes gruff. Perhaps one of our children comes up to us and speaks very nicely to us but we're having a hard day, so we grump at them. That's human nature. And the child, of course, is hurt, backs off, and says, "I'm going to wait until Dad or Mom feels better before I go back into that tiger trap again."

But this is how it is.

THE GIFTS OF LOVE

The gifts of God come to us most often through other people. And the gift of love often comes through us to other people. If we let it; if we open our heart. And it must be with discrimination.

Love those who are close to you with your whole heart, but love those who are outside of your close circle with a detached love, with charity. In other words, you cannot love everyone with the same warmth. Loving means acting and showing your love. The human body can give only so much love and usually we reserve the warm love for those who are close to us. And they do the same for us, their loved one.

Love does everything for those it loves.

Love does everything for those it loves. In a relationship it isn't like the man gives 50 percent and the woman gives 50 percent. It doesn't work like that.

You have to give 100 percent of yourself. And expect no praise or no reward for it.

So you just love. And why do you love? Because you love.

When I was back in high school, some friends of mine used to sing this inane song. It went like this: "We're here because we're here because we're here because we're here." And they'd go on and on. They'd wander off down the hall, singing this song. And it made perfect sense to me then because I didn't know why I was here. And they didn't know either.

So, it's that way with love too. We love because we love because we love because we love.

Because it's the nature of an open consciousness. To simply love and give of God's love to other people. But even more important is to receive it. To receive the blessings that are all around us.

HELPING THE CAUSE OF ECK

Many people have found that when they are working in the cause of Divine Spirit little miracles happen. Things come to make something work better for you.

We have many ECK members in Africa, Europe, Australia, and other places around the world. There's a bond among us. There's this line of communication among us.

A Nigerian ECKist used to do a lot of things in the early years of Eckankar in Africa. He'd give introductory talks. And he found that when he was helping in the cause of ECK, often miracles would come, a knowingness about things.

One time he was to give an introductory talk, and he was making a poster. He had a whole bunch of posters to make. It was going to take a long time. He was thinking, *I wish my friend were here to help me with these posters. Otherwise I'm going to be at this all day.*

As he was seated at the table in his apartment working on the posters, suddenly his Spiritual Eye opened and he saw his friend walking up the stairs to his apartment. "Maybe it's my imagination," the ECKist said. But he got up and went to the door. He opened the door just as his friend arrived.

It is similar to when you call somebody, the phone doesn't ring, but they pick it up and say, "Hello?" Here was the friend at the door, the door suddenly opened in front of him, and the ECKist said, "Come on in. I've been expecting you." For at least twenty seconds.

SOMETHING EXTRA FROM DIVINE SPIRIT

This ECKist mentioned that he noticed what happens when people help in the cause of ECK: There is a return from Divine Spirit to help things out.

He and another member of Eckankar were to go to a faraway city in Nigeria to be guest speakers at an Eckankar seminar. So they got in the car. They drove all day. They got there just about midnight. The people in that city had reserved a hotel room for them; but when they arrived, it was after midnight. They got to the gate of the hotel, and the security guard wouldn't let them in. "Nobody gets in after midnight," he said.

And so now the two ECKists are in a strange city, and they're wondering where they're going to stay.

The cab left. They were just standing out there in the dark. One of them says, "I know an ECKist here, but he lives about an hour away. So we might as well start walking."

When people help in the cause of ECK there is a return from Divine Spirit to help things out.

They start walking, and it's getting close to one o'clock in the morning. They're out in the middle of the street. Suddenly a car comes driving up in the dark. It stops, the driver looks out the window and says to the two ECKists, "Get in." So they get in. The driver turns out to be another ECKist.

This ECKist had been at a party when suddenly he got this nudge to just get up and leave. So he got up and left. And the Mahanta gave him a nudge to drive down certain streets. He didn't know why he was out driving down those dark streets.

As he's driving, he comes to this particular street off in a deserted part of the city. And here he sees these two men walking along. He gets a nudge to pull up and invite them to get in. Then they find out that they're all ECKists and that these two are the guest speakers for the seminar that weekend.

In this way, the two ECKists were taken care of. The ECKist said later that he had so many assurances of Divine Spirit helping him while he was helping the cause of ECK. It gave him a lot of courage to do more things for ECK.

The stories that happen in Eckankar today are very similar to the stories that happened way back at the beginning of Christianity.

EARLY STORIES

The stories that happen in Eckankar today are very similar to the stories that happened way back at the beginning of Christianity. The same sorts of stories and miracles are still going on today.

But this is not why we're here. We're not here to stand around in a group where everybody sees little tongues like as of fire on their heads, and one asks, "Oh, what is this?" And someone else says, "Why, I don't know. You'd think our hair would burn off but it seems to be holding out OK."

When this happened in biblical times, nobody

explained to these people what was going on. No one asked, "What are those little flames coming up in your head?" And no one explained, "Well, that's a sign of the Holy Spirit."

It was all new to them. Most of this happened when Christianity was still coming out of the nest from the Jewish religion. All the early Christians were Jews. We forget that today. But Christ was a Jew; the early Christians were Jews. It was their world. It wasn't bad. It was just people, doing bad things to one of their own members who didn't happen to fit in. It happens all the time.

PAST-LIFE INFORMATION

Sometimes Divine Spirit will give you an insight into something that's happening in your daily life. And one of the most interesting ways is through an experience of a past life.

We have people in ECK who come from all religious faiths—Christianity, Hinduism, Islam, and many others. And every religion has its own view about how Soul exists, when Soul began, and the final destination of Soul. Every group has its own beliefs. But by the time people come to Eckankar, they've usually been introduced to the concept of reincarnation.

Reincarnation is very popular nowadays. On TV they can do some marvelous reenactments with computer graphics of what they think flying saucers and reincarnation and all these things should look like. They can play it up with lights and auras.

But it's not nearly as glorious as the spiritual experience itself.

Sometimes Divine Spirit will give you an insight into something that's happening in your daily life.

THE MOST BEAUTIFUL BLUE LIGHT

An ECKist who works in the nuclear field described the core of a nuclear reactor. He said the light is such a beautiful blue that it strongly affects anyone who sees it. It's because the atom is showing its color as the nuclear reaction's going on.

The atom is a building block of the physical universe. It's not unusual for people to see blue both in a nuclear reactor and also on the inner planes, because the atom goes even further than the physical plane.

There's substance and structure on all levels up to the Soul Plane. And beyond that point, there is no more of the mixture of matter and spirit which makes up the buildings and the bodies of the inhabitants who live there.

But the blue light is very, very special.

There's substance and structure on all levels up to the Soul Plane.

INSIGHT INTO ANOTHER LIFE

A group of students from Ghana went outside their country for a year's study of French. Ghana's a French-speaking country, and these students wanted to become more fluent in French.

One of the girls, a black student, happened to meet a white German man. And just like that, they were close friends.

All her friends started to talk. "Got a romance going here?" they asked her. "What's going on? And why with a white man?" There's this thing between races. When someone of a different color comes into the established race of a community, it's sometimes a problem. People raise their eyebrows, and friends become upset. It happens all the time.

Her friends began to talk about her and say some untrue things about her friendship with this white

German. The girl didn't want to give up her friends from Ghana, but she didn't want to give up her new friend either.

She was trying to figure out how to balance all this. So one day she decided to do a spiritual exercise.

It's very simple. You just shut your eyes, and you talk to your spiritual guide—whoever you feel very comfortable with. It can be Jesus or whomever. In Eckankar people look to the Mahanta.

The girl said, "Please, Wah Z, give me an insight into what's happening. I don't know what's going on. I don't want to lose my friends on this side; I don't want to lose my friend on that side." This was basically the problem she was trying to resolve.

The next thing she knew, she found herself in another lifetime, standing on a beach with a baby in her arms. Just offshore was one of the early slaving ships, and the white slavers were standing on the beach. They had whips. A whole line of black slaves was also on the beach, and they were tied together with chains.

A point of interest here: so often one race gets upset at another race and says, "You did these cruel things to us." But many of the people who were sold into slavery in Africa were actually prisoners of war of some other black tribe. And the black tribe had a choice: either kill them or sell them for some kind of money so that they could enrich themselves. And I don't know if the prisoners were lucky or not, but sometimes instead of being killed outright, their black captors sold them into slavery. They would bring them from the interior of the continent where the whites did not go. This is where the fighting went on. And then the blacks would bring out the captives and sell them to the slavers, and the slavers would

You just shut your eyes, and you talk to your spiritual guide— whoever you feel very comfortable with.

send them on ships off to North or South America.

But history sometimes gets a little cloudy. People revise it as time goes on. We like to think that another race did this all to us when actually our own people did it to us. This happens a lot.

In this woman's past-life experience, she saw the white slavers loading blacks onto the ships, and she was standing there crying with a child in her arms. Her husband was one of the slaves. So she went to the slave masters and begged them, "Please let my husband go. We have a child." And of course they laughed at her and ignored her.

Pretty soon it was time for the last line of slaves to board the ship, and as they're going on, the husband calls to his wife standing on shore. He says, "If we don't get to meet again in this lifetime, surely we will meet in another."

And so the ECKist from Ghana realized that it wasn't just mere chance that she happened to have run into this white German student and have such a strong attraction to him. She began to notice that whenever she saw her German friend, he would act just like an African. He walked and talked and did other things just like an African. She used to look at him and wonder, *Where did you pick that up?*

As this inner experience was coming to an end, the Mahanta said to her, "Your friend in this lifetime was your husband in that lifetime." All of a sudden she understood why there was such a strong rapport between them.

After this, she was able to handle her friends better when they tried to intimidate her by saying, "You shouldn't be seen with that white man. What will people think?" This is the social consciousness speaking. It's one element of the human conscious-

The Mahanta said to her, "Your friend in this lifetime was your husband in that lifetime."

ness that tries to keep everybody at the same level. You don't want someone taller standing out in a crowd. So the social consciousness tries to make everybody the same level. But after her inner experience she was able to be firm with her friends because she knew what she was doing and she knew why. She knew this man was a very dear person from another lifetime, and this is just how it was.

So the woman was able to go forward with her life and straighten everything out, keep her friends on both sides, and resolve this problem. She was able to resolve this problem by seeing the past life. It explained so much about their close affinity and why he acted like an African.

UNDERSTANDING OF SOUL

Soul is immortal. It has no beginning nor ending.

I try to give you the very best examples I can of experiences people have in Eckankar. Sometimes you won't have a past-life experience at all. I know in my early years in ECK I had a lot of them. Some of them were pleasant. There were some unpleasant ones, where you find that you are leaving a certain existence under certain conditions. And you don't like the experience at all.

But you get an understanding about yourself. You learn about yourself as Soul. Soul is immortal. It has no beginning nor ending.

The definition in Eckankar of Soul as an immortal being is a true one. Soul is created before and beyond time and space. Christians believe that Soul is born or created at conception. This causes a lot of problems.

If you believe Soul is born within the realm of time and space, you can't really say It's without a beginning. It has a beginning in time and space, if you're going to look at it that way. But God created Soul before the worlds began. And then Soul merely comes here as part of Its experience from the other worlds beyond time and space. It comes here and has many, many lifetimes learning one thing or another.

The greatest thing Soul learns is how to love God. Our experiences teach us how to love God.

What We're Here For

Basically the greatest thing Soul learns is how to love God. Our experiences teach us how to love God.

And how do we learn this? Through loving ourselves or through loving others. With some people the first step in loving God comes in loving other people. And until you love yourself, you cannot truly love other people.

You may get along very well with other people. Often these are people who are strongly driven by the mind. They get along well with everybody else but love has not yet touched their heart. Because when love touches your heart, you become quite a different person.

A New Leaf

People have asked me from time to time why the Higher Initiates in ECK are called the Brothers of the Leaf. I really haven't talked about it. *The Shariyat-Ki-Sugmad,* our bible, mentions the term only once, I believe. So people ask me, "Why are the Fifth Initiates and higher called the Brothers of the Leaf?"

Basically it's because when someone comes to the Soul Plane and becomes established there, he should turn a new leaf.

Paul Twitchell, the founder of Eckankar, began speaking of the Brothers of the Leaf. He had a connection at one point with the Catholic Church, and he knew how powerful some of the fraternal orders were in accomplishing good things. He could see the potential power of the Brothers of the Leaf working together to accomplish a common spiritual goal.

My dad was a farmer, and he would drive us home from church. To the north of our place was a woods, and there was a ledge farther to the north all covered with trees. When the leaves turned white, Dad would say, "See those leaves up there? They're not green; they're white. It means it's going to rain."

When Soul turns a new leaf, it's like turning from green—which means concern with the things of the earth—to white—which are the things of Divine Spirit.

When the leaf turns white, it really has turned itself upward and open like a cup. It means that Soul is ready to receive the blessings of the Holy Spirit raining down from God. And this is a fuller explanation of the Brothers of the Leaf.

It's basically the creed of the Three Musketeers: All for one, one for all. When people reach the Fifth Plane but do not act with this love and giving, and do not act like vehicles for God's love to others, it proves that they haven't turned a new leaf.

So when people ask me, "What does it mean to be a member of the Brothers of the Leaf?" it's someone who spiritually has turned a new leaf and is now open to the blessings of God flowing down like a wave. Like a wave from heaven. And it takes something to open up to that.

Soul is ready to receive the blessings of the Holy Spirit raining down from God. And this is a fuller explanation of the Brothers of the Leaf.

BUDDIES

I'm looking along a couple pages in my notes here. My handwriting is always very careful, like an accountant's, because I write slowly. Whenever I wrote fast—from grade school on—it was illegible. Teachers would complain. Everybody would complain that they couldn't read it. But when I took my time, I would win penmanship awards.

One time in our grade school we had a penmanship contest. There were only two of us in sixth grade. I had very neat handwriting, and my cousin Jerry didn't. So I'd usually win the award. But we were buddies, and this time he said, "I want one too. Will you write the test out for me?" And so with my own handwriting I wrote the little test out for him.

The teacher knew our handwriting. And he said to Jerry, while looking at me, "You sure that's your handwriting?"

Jerry said, "Yes, I'm sure."

But the difference was as different as our looks. I had dark hair, Jerry had blond hair. Our handwriting was just as unique as our appearance. But we were buddies. We would do anything and everything for each other. So I gave him my handwriting because he got a piece of paper for it and it seemed to make everyone happy.

His handwriting never did improve after that. And mine never got any better, either.

Paul Twitchell founded Eckankar in 1965.

REMEMBERING

Paul Twitchell founded Eckankar in 1965. October 1995 will be our thirtieth anniversary. I don't know how much we'll say about it: We spend most of our time in the present. We don't go too much into the historical thing.

Some people dwell on the past. Like me, for instance. I have this thing about being able to remember things all the way back—people, events, experiences.

My wife looks at me, sort of puzzled, because to her that's like a past life—a far distant past life. She often says, "Why do you remember all those things?"

I say, "Because I can't help it."

I just remember things. Not just in the past, in the present too. It gets to be quite a burden to people who have to listen to me talk about the past. Like my wife. But she's nice. She'll say, "Oh, isn't that the story where so and so . . . ?" I say, "I guess you've heard that ten times, haven't you?" But she's sweet. She never says yes or no. She just smiles and loves me anyway.

HELP FROM ECK MASTERS

Paul Twitchell brought out the teachings of Eckankar back in 1965, and then he translated, or died, in 1971.

Sometimes when the ECK Masters have a close working relationship with some of the members of Eckankar, the students will see them again. For instance, Rebazar Tarzs is an ECK Master who worked years ago on the Earth Plane as spiritual leader of Eckankar before it was known as Eckankar. He had a number of students who came into this lifetime, and sometimes those students may see him. He'll give them advice about how to do certain things to meet certain problems in daily living.

Or it may be one of the other ECK Masters who will be working with some students from the past—sometimes where a student gained very much spiritually but for some reason or other left ECK.

These Masters all work with me as the spiritual leader of the current times. And they work with all these people. But when they have a special person they were working with in the past and there is danger, they'll come to help.

Rebazar Tarzs is an ECK Master who worked years ago on the Earth Plane as spiritual leader of Eckankar before it was known as Eckankar.

A woman wrote me about an experience that happened in 1983, twelve years after Paul Twitchell died.

EXPERIENCE WITH PAUL TWITCHELL

A woman wrote me about an experience that happened in 1983, twelve years after Paul Twitchell died.

The woman had this beautiful beach home. Her mother lived next door. It was a duplex. And her mother had a trailer for sale. Right in front of the duplex was the sign "Trailer for Sale."

One day it was raining very, very hard. The young woman's daughter was playing on the floor. Her daughter was only two at the time. The woman decided to take a shower and clean up while her daughter was playing in the living room.

The woman had just gotten into Eckankar, and she had a bunch of ECK books on the coffee table; some more were stacked on top of the refrigerator.

While she was in the shower, she heard a man's voice in the living room. So she turned the shower off, put on a towel, and went out there. And she saw this man. "Can I help you?" she asked him. It was one of those very awkward situations. Yet she didn't feel afraid of him for some reason.

He said, "Your daughter let me in." A two-year-old girl unlocked the screen door and let a strange man walk in? But the man said again, "Your daughter let me in. And I was talking to her."

He was asking about the trailer out front. And the woman said, "That's my mother's. You'll have to come back tomorrow or some other time when she's here. I'm taking a shower right now, and I think it would be better if you came back another day." He said, "OK." And he left. But as he was leaving, she noticed that it was still pouring rain outside. She didn't have a porch or any kind of landing whatsoever. To get inside from a car, he should have been soaked. He should have been drenched. He was perfectly dry.

The woman was looking at this, just thinking about all the things that didn't quite fit. She saw the man to the door, locked the door, and went back to her bedroom to dress. She was just about ready to forget this experience but when she came out into the living room, her two-year-old daughter took one of the ECK books, *The Tiger's Fang*—which Paul Twitchell had written—and turned it over.

On the back cover was the picture of the same man who had just been in the living room. And she said, "That was Paul Twitchell."

The man's been dead for twelve years, she thought. And she can't figure this out.

TRANSLATION

We in ECK don't say *dead* because that's so final. It means the end. We say *translated.* It means like translating a language from English into German or German into English or French.

The meaning and the content and the essence is the same. In other words, Soul is the same and can carry Its body of knowledge from one lifetime into another. For most people, it's an unconscious transfer of knowledge.

But the ECK Masters can remember things that are necessary for them from the past as they give up one body for another through other lifetimes as is necessary.

Soul is the same and can carry Its body of knowledge from one lifetime into another.

MESSAGE FROM AN ECK MASTER

That night the little girl had a hard time going to sleep. She cried and cried. The mother had to get up. And pretty soon the grandmother came over to console the little girl. But the girl cried most of the night.

Finally when morning came, none of the family had gotten any rest. They decided they might as well go out and try to get some breakfast.

During the night when the grandmother had come over, she had looked over at the heater. It was plugged into the wall. And she had a sudden feeling there was something wrong with that heater. And so she had unplugged it for the night.

The little girl had spent the whole night crying about something. At age two, she couldn't say, "I think something very bad's going to happen because that nice man who was here today told me and he told me tonight in my dreams too. And that's why I'm crying." Two-year-olds can't really express themselves that well. But they can cry, and so the little girl cried.

So they all got dressed and left for breakfast. While they were gone, the duplex burned down.

When the fire inspector came later, he said that the reason for the fire was the faulty heater. If the grandmother hadn't unplugged it, the heater would have caught that old wooden building on fire during the night. It's unlikely that they would have gotten out alive.

They realized that this ECK Master was indeed very much alive and working in the Soul body, appearing to those with whom he was very close. The baby, who is now a teenager, had been with him before. And so he had come to her to protect her.

This ECK Master was indeed very much alive and working in the Soul body, appearing to those with whom he was very close.

AWARENESS OF LOVE AND PROTECTION

This is another area of gratitude. When we speak of opening your wings, it's coming into an awareness of the spiritual love and protection of the ECK Masters.

They are the guardian angels around you all the time. It's just a matter of opening your awareness and going above the human consciousness to recognize and benefit from this.

Often you benefit anyway because most people benefit from the protection and the love without even knowing about it. Only later do they come to this realization and recognition of God's love showering down upon them.

I'd like to close this evening with the blessing of the ECK Masters: May the blessings be.

When we speak of opening your wings, it's coming into an awareness of the spiritual love and protection of the ECK Masters.

ECK Summer Festival, Anaheim, California, Saturday, June 17, 1995

"What's your secret? How can you make life go so well even though it's tiring us out?" He said, "Dancing to the rhythm of life. Dancing to the rhythm of life."

9

Dancing to the Rhythm of Life

*H*ealth is part of the spiritual life. Because one of the highest qualities of Soul is survival.

Someone asked an Eighth Initiate, "Do you choose the time of your passing from this plane to the next?" In other words, the time you leave here. As if it would really be something to choose the time to go. But I think it's a greater attribute to exercise every bit of your creativity to survive no matter where you are.

If you try to shortcut here, then you're going to go into the next life. And what are you going to do there? Try to shortcut there too and not exercise your full potential to survive.

The whole thing about Soul is survival, of course. And then you find out what makes it worthwhile is learning how to love.

Taking care of our health is certainly one of the strongest aspects of survival here. This is why it's an important part of the ECK teachings.

I was very sick last year. Many people gave me information about health and healing, and whenever I could, I sorted through it and passed back to

The whole thing about Soul is survival. Taking care of our health is certainly one of the strongest aspects of survival here.

Even in our
health, we find
that we are
each very
unique.

you anything that seemed to be of some worth to the most people. But some of the gadgets and devices I tried made me very ill. So I do not recommend them, but I don't say anything against them either because they have helped some people and they will continue to help some people. Even in our health, we find that we are each very unique.

HOT SPOT

Yesterday my wife and I ate in a restaurant for the first time in nearly a year and a half. And it was very interesting. I generally take along a meter that measures electromagnetic radiation. In the restaurant, we sat in a booth, and the reading was high: There was a fair amount of electromagnetic radiation nearby. But we were with some other people, and my attention was away from my health and on them. After we'd been there for about an hour, I could feel a burn, like a sunburn.

I took the meter out again and tested spots in the rest of the restaurant. It was electromagnetically cool, except for our booth. I had walked straight to the hottest area in the whole place and sat down. It was set up like a trick. These things always are. Little traps.

It turned out that there was a neon sign in the window next to our booth. It was behind a curtain, so you couldn't see it. I was getting a high reading in the booth, and when I put the meter next to the sign, the needle went right off the scale.

I'd been sitting there for an hour, so all the symptoms came back—the early warning ones—which told me that I still have a way to go with healing. I found out I wasn't as strong as I thought I was. I have gained a lot, but I have a long way to go.

I'm already looking ahead to the next seminar, wondering if I can make it. Airplanes have high levels of electromagnetic radiation.

But I try to pass along the things that I've learned and the best things that come from you.

NEW RESEARCH INTO HEALTH

I had mentioned a book by Hulda Clark, a cancer researcher. She's not a medical doctor. She's in alternative medicine, and in her practice she's noticed something. In all the cancer cases that have come to her attention, there were usually two elements: The presence of a human intestinal fluke and propyl alcohol in the person's system. If both these were present, often the person had cancer.

Other people are now researching her findings, checking to see whether or not there is actually a connection.

You wonder why it hasn't been discovered before. If it's as obvious as human intestinal flukes and propyl alcohol, someone else should have found this long ago.

A researcher wrote a review of Clark's book. He studies parasites, and he said that in people who are tested for parasites, after about two hours this human intestinal fluke does not show up in the test. The patient brings his stool sample into the lab, but by the time the doctor gets it under a microscope, the human intestinal flukes no longer show up. So that may be a new area for medical researchers who want to look into this further and see if they can indeed find a way to give people a better chance at life.

Dancing to the rhythm of life is our theme, and basically the search for health is just that.

Dancing to the rhythm of life is our theme this morning, and basically the search for health is just that. If we are in tune with life, then everything will work pretty well.

THE WAYS WE LEARN SPIRITUALLY

In my position as spiritual leader of Eckankar I find I have to go through the mill. I always have. I seem to learn better that way. I know that we all like things to be pleasant. But when things get hard, that's often when we learn the best. Because we've got more at stake: our well-being, our peace of mind, and our concern about those who depend on us.

When we get sick, it can make us a little bit more aware of the rhythm of life, of dancing to the rhythm of life. We say, "Hmm, I definitely know today that something's wrong."

The funny thing about the dance of life is that when we're in it—when everything's going right—we're least aware of it. This is the great paradox. When everything's going right and we're in the rhythm of life, we're the least aware of it.

This is why sickness is often such a great spiritual aid. First of all, the illness is signaling something. It's saying, "The way to health and happiness is that way, and apparently you're not going that way. So, sit up and take note."

If you have the same recurring illness all the time, it's worth it to use your creative powers to find out what is causing this and what you can do to try to make your life better—to come to some kind of conclusion about this.

HOW IT BEGINS

Back in 1991, there was an attempt to keep me from celebrating the tenth anniversary of being the

---

When everything's going right and we're in the rhythm of life, we're the least aware of it.

spiritual leader of Eckankar. All the different negative forces came together to try to stop me completely.
I took a trip to Africa that year, and all the inocu-
lations for the trip were quite poisonous to my body.
Right after I got home, I was stung by bees — something which hadn't bothered me before but sure did
this time. And two days later, I got into a car accident.

Right after that came the ECK Worldwide Seminar. It went on and on and on like this.

I got sicker and sicker. I stayed home nearly all
the time. I had some internal injuries, but I just kept
trying to do my work and not bother anyone else. I'd
come to the seminar, take the neck brace off in the
car, come out onstage, and give the talk. My back was
really burning by the time I got offstage. Until that
time, I really hadn't had any experience with whip-
lash. But I happened to have a good case of it.

Over the next couple of years, my body got weaker
and weaker. That opened the door for sensitivity to
electromagnetic radiation. I would like to overcome
this someday too, and I'm working on it step-by-step.
But I suspect it's a little bit like a sunburn. Once you
get a really bad sunburn, it takes a while before you
lose your sensitivity to the sun.

GAINING DISCRIMINATION

We are in a highly electronic society today. If it
weren't for many of these wonderful inventions like
the microphone, I'd have to be speaking a lot louder
or the rooms would have to be designed to carry the
human voice better. We're in a different world entirely from just a couple of generations ago. And the
human body hasn't adapted very quickly.

Some of you are very strong. Others of you have
a number of allergies and complaints that are

We are in a highly electronic society today. And the human body hasn't adapted very quickly.

As you grow in discrimination, you learn you can only accept a certain amount of something. You fall back on your creativity—the creativity of Soul.

probably aggravated by the twentieth century and all its innovations.

These innovations help in so many ways. And yet, we have to see how much we can handle, we have to be very selective.

Another ECK quality that we develop is discrimination. And as you grow in discrimination, you learn you can only accept a certain amount of something. Then you have to step back and say, "I'll learn to do things another way." You fall back on your creativity—the creativity of Soul.

DANCING TO THE RHYTHM OF LIFE

Throughout the process of healing, I try to level out the ups and downs of life. I try to take things in stride.

One of the ECKists had a dream about an old ECK Master. He was going up a steep mountain with this chela and several other ECKists. *Chela* simply means "spiritual student." The ECKists would run up the mountain ahead of the old Master, then they'd get to a rock, sit down, and rest by a little tree. Pretty soon the Master would come along; his pace was slow and deliberate. And he'd keep right on going, moving very steadily up the mountain. So then the students would jump up again and race up the mountain.

They'd sometimes run a little bit, and then they'd walk fast. Again they'd get ahead of the Master and sit down. Pretty soon here came the old Master again, slow and patient. He kept right on going, smiling and happy; his energy seemed good.

And when the spiritual students had rested, they jumped up again. When they finally got to the top of this mountain, they were exhausted. Very shortly the old ECK Master arrived at the top, smiling and walking very steadily. He had a good pace and rhythm.

One woman asked him, "What's your secret? How can you make life go so well even though it's tiring us out?"

He said, "Dancing to the rhythm of life. Dancing to the rhythm of life."

But before you can dance to the rhythm of life, you have to be aware that there is a rhythm. You have to know when you have bumped into the fence on the left or the fence on the right. And you have to know when you have broken right through the fence and gone completely off the path.

Before you can dance to the rhythm of life, you have to be aware that there is a rhythm.

The Stupid Cow

At home on the farm we had fences around the grain fields. At first we had ordinary wire fences, and then Dad put up electric fences. It gave the cows a little less incentive to push through and eat the grain in the next field.

But some of the cows got smart. They began to bump the other cows into the fence. And they usually bumped the stupid cows.

Cows have personalities. There are the smart ones, and there are the not-so-smart ones. The not-so-smart ones would stand by a fence that was pretty well broken down except for this one wire of electricity which was supposed to hold them back. Normally it would, unless a stupid cow crashed through it. So that's what the smart cows did. They'd push the stupid cow through. And the stupid cow would get the shock. Once the electric fence fell down, it shorted out. And that was the end of the electric fence. The other cows would just walk over it into the other field.

The stupid cow would stand by this fence chewing her cud, thinking of heaven knows what. The smart cows would be standing off to the side saying, "Little bit more to the left." And then one of the smart cows would run, head down, into the side of the stupid cow and knock the wind out of her. You could just hear the cow go, "Hoo-oo-oo!"

The rest of the herd would walk through the fence into the field of oats or corn.

> We have to learn not to let other people push us through the fence.

WE NEED TO WATCH OUT TOO

We have to learn not to let other people push us through the fence. If we know what our diet is — maybe we can't handle sugar very well — and someone else says, "Would you like some ice cream on your pie?" we have to know that pie alone or ice cream alone is OK. Two of them together is like running into the electric fence.

After she hits the electric fence a couple of times, even the most stupid cow gets a little bit smarter. Often she still stood by the fence, but she wasn't chewing her cud as contentedly as before. She was looking around, watching the other cows.

You don't always figure out the first time that maybe pie and ice cream are too much for you. But after you eat them together a couple of times and you run into the electric fence, it slowly dawns on you. Then you say, "Well, I'll take half servings." Or, as I know some people do, you take some desert from somebody else that is sitting there. Then it doesn't count.

It's aggravating for those of you who are really hungry. You order your dessert. Your mate says, "No, I don't want any, thank you. I'm watching my weight." And the next thing you know, your dessert's all gone.

A friend of mine had a girlfriend who was very thin. She was always concerned about putting on too much weight, which seemed ridiculous because she was so thin. She always complained, "I eat like a bird, and I still put on weight." One day he finally said to her, "Eat like a bird? You eat like a vulture." You find you're not exactly in the rhythm of life with your mate when you say that in front of other people. There were hard feelings.

Gratitude is the secret of love.

WHEN WE GIVE LOVE

Gratitude is the secret of love, and often Divine Spirit brings up situations for us, where we purposely have to wait and wait and wait. *Why?* we wonder. *Because the Holy Spirit likes to see me wait in lines or something? Is this the whole purpose of spiritual lessons?*

An ECKist from Germany was just starting out in the workforce, and she was having to watch her money very carefully. So throughout the month, she worked here and there, doing odd jobs. She was able to save some money in an envelope at home to take care of rent and her utility bills. At the end of each month, she went to the bank to pay her bills.

One day there was a line of people ahead of her at the bank. The cashier taking care of the bills was known to be very, very slow. She was very slow this particular day too. It took one hour for her to process one customer.

By this time, most of the people in line were thinking, *There must be a better way to do this.* All the other customers were getting angry and impatient. And the ECKist was too, at first, and then she remembered: There must be something to learn here.

"Maybe I will just quietly give love to this woman. She's very, very slow but she's careful, and she doesn't make mistakes," the ECKist said to herself.

The ECKist always put a certain amount of money in a kitty. Each month she'd bring 750 deutsche marks—a two-hundred-deutsche-mark bill, five one hundreds, and a fifty—to the bank. This was how she gathered her money together. But she never needed to use the two-hundred-deutsche-mark bill because the rest covered her bills each month. After she paid her bills, she would put any remaining money back in the kitty, and as she worked throughout the month, she would keep adding to her kitty. The two-hundred-deutsche-mark bill that she never touched was always special, but she took it along to the bank just in case the expenses that month were higher than she expected.

The line took forever, but she finally got to the cashier. She handed her envelope to the woman, and the woman went to look at the accounting.

"You've paid me too much," she told the ECKist when she returned.

The ECKist had just become a Second Initiate, and she was thinking of giving a donation to the Temple of ECK in Minneapolis. But she didn't have the money because her budget was very tight.

So when the cashier said, "You gave me too much money," the ECKist thought it was the two-hundred-deutsche-mark bill. But the cashier said, "You've given me this five-hundred-deutsche-mark bill, and it's too much." "No, that's not possible," the ECKist said. "I never had a five-hundred-deutsche-mark bill in this envelope."

"Well, look," the cashier said. "I haven't even taken the money out of my hand yet. It's right here." And the ECKist looked, and there it was. Somehow she had ended up with much more, a considerable sum—

The ECKist was thinking of giving a donation to the Temple of ECK in Minneapolis.

about what she paid for her rent and utilities each month.

Because she had given love to someone, even though the cashier was very, very slow, somehow by the grace of ECK, this money had multiplied for her.

Maybe the money would have been there even if she hadn't given love to the cashier. But she did give love, and the money was there. And so she was able to give a donation to the Temple of ECK, even though she had very little.

What is the rhythm of life? Showing divine love for other people. This is being in the rhythm of life, as we see with this German ECKist.

KEEPING YOUR WORD

Sometimes dancing to the rhythm of life means learning to keep our word. We've talked before about the two laws of Richard Maybury, who wrote *Whatever Happened to Justice?* One of the laws is, "Do all you have agreed to do."

Even though it's a verbal contract and everything isn't signed by lawyers on either side, if you've given your word, follow through on your obligations until the conditions change so that conditions are outside what the original contract was.

A man had a good job, and one day he got a better offer from a large computer company. It was a much better offer. So he gave his resignation to his employer. As he was about to leave this company and take the new job, he got a second offer—many times better and higher in pay than the one he had just accepted. Now he didn't know what to do.

He knew that the Maybury law says, "Do all you have agreed to do." And he had given his verbal acceptance of this new position.

Sometimes dancing to the rhythm of life means learning to keep our word.

His current supervisor was his friend. So he talked to his friend about this. "Do you think it would be ethical if I told the people who gave me the first offer that I couldn't accept it?" the man asked his friend. Of course he wouldn't tell them that he had gotten a better offer.

The friend said, "It depends upon what your goals are, what you want out of life. There wasn't a written contract." It sounded as if the supervisor thought it was OK to back out of the contract. Then Divine Spirit had the supervisor do something that was completely out of the ordinary and very insignificant at the time. There was an acorn lying on the sidewalk, and his supervisor just bent over and picked it up. He said to the man, "Here. Plant this. And it will grow into a large oak."

Keeping his word was more important than $20,000 because he was building for the future.

The ECKist realized that his friend was being a vehicle for the Holy Spirit in giving him this waking dream. In showing the ECKist this little acorn, he was saying, "It will grow, if you plant it. It will grow into a large oak." The oak represented integrity.

Even though the other job offered him $20,000 more a year he didn't accept it because he was planting this oak of integrity in his life. Keeping his word was more important than $20,000 because he was building for the future. He was building for his spiritual future, not just here but in the inner worlds.

As I mentioned before, someone asked an Eighth Initiate, "Do you choose your time to leave earth?" Almost as if it's a quick exit from your responsibilities here on earth. You don't want to do that. You want to exercise all your creative power and survive no matter where you are. As Paul in the New Testament said, "In whatsoever state I am, therewith to be content."

INSIGHTS INTO LIFE

Sometimes we learn about the rhythm of life through the Spiritual Exercises of ECK which give us an insight into ourselves. They answer the questions Why are we always bumping into the electric fence? Why are we always straying off the path?

A woman had been in ECK fifteen years and had never had much luck with visualization techniques. She never had Soul Travel or dream experiences of this nature during this time. She tried different visualization techniques from the ECK discourses, but she had no luck. So she finally gave up. "I'm going to do it real simple," she said. "I'm just going to visualize the Inner Master's face and sing HU."

And something happened. She began to get insights into life that she never had before.

She still didn't have dreams, and she still didn't have Soul Travel experiences; but she was starting to get insights into her own life.

One morning she was having breakfast, listening to the radio. A very beautiful classical piece of music came on, and as she listened to it, she suddenly realized an answer to the one of the problems she'd been having her whole life in her relationships with men.

She'd always had this feeling that she was inferior to a man, and after a while she'd begin considering herself a slave to the relationship. Finally, she would just become filled with disgust at herself, and she'd break off the relationship.

This had left her very unhappy. For many years she had wondered what she could do about it.

And as she was having breakfast, this insight suddenly came through, simply that she was Soul.

Sometimes we learn about the rhythm of life through the Spiritual Exercises of ECK which give us an insight into ourselves.

She was neither male nor female, but Soul, a spark of God. And if she could remember that, she could regard other people as Soul too, as a spiritual part of God. And once she did this, she found that her life had changed.

She had in fact turned a new leaf.

LOSING AN OLD HABIT

If we've started a habit of any kind—anger, drinking, smoking, greed, lust—sometimes Divine Spirit will take these things away immediately.

Things don't usually change overnight, because habits of the human consciousness are very hard to break. If we've started a habit of any kind—anger, drinking, smoking, greed, lust—sometimes Divine Spirit will take these things away immediately. Sometimes they just go away. People lose the desire for alcohol or cigarettes overnight. Other people continue to fight with it. They may get rid of the desire to smoke cigarettes, but alcohol hangs on and on and on. Eventually the problem either goes away or it doesn't—depending upon that person's spiritual unfoldment.

That's why this concept of Soul being a unique creation of God is so important. That's why it's one of the central teachings of Eckankar.

It's not a question of being right or wrong about health or smoking and drinking. But is it good for you spiritually? Does it hurt other people? In healing, some methods did not work for me, but other things worked very well. And some that won't work for me will work for others.

There are all kinds of studies now that show that secondhand smoke does hurt people. I think the only studies that show it doesn't hurt other people are studies funded by the tobacco companies. But that's just my observation.

A STRONG BOND

Sometimes there's a strong bond between people and their pets, or a bond with certain other people. And we wonder, *Why such a strong bond?* Often the answer lies in a past life.

If we had the ability through a dream experience, Soul Travel, or the intuitive powers of Soul to understand this connection between that other Soul and ourselves, it would clear up so many things. It would let us treat other people with more love and kindness, because we have an insight into our relationship with them.

One of the members of Eckankar wrote to me about her cat, Misha. This Siamese cat just wants to love. Eat too, but mostly love. Cats generally want to eat first and love second. And Siamese cats can be very finicky and self-centered. But not Misha.

When the ECKist was sleeping in the morning, the cat would lie very, very still. Most cats are different: as soon as the cat's awake and hungry, it starts moving around, maybe licking your face. "Breakfast time. Let's get up and go outside." They will be a nuisance. But not Misha.

Misha also had a habit of jumping into the woman's arms, just wanting to be loving. And after she got hugged and loved, it was time for breakfast. But loving always came first. Misha was a very smart cat, a very advanced Soul.

In ECK, we do regard our pets as Soul. Why? Because they are.

PETS ARE VEHICLES OF LOVE

People who are new to Eckankar are sometimes surprised when they hear us refer to cats and dogs as Soul. In ECK, we do regard our pets as Soul. Why? Because they are.

They're a creation of God—just as surely as we are. And when a cat translates, or dies, something leaves just as surely as when a human being dies. And when a baby takes its first breath of life, something comes in. This happens just as surely as in a kitten.

Human vanity likes to say, "God made us and put a Soul in us," as if you can possess Soul. But in Eckankar, we say, "We are Soul." We are Soul, and through successive lifetimes, we take on a body for whatever experience we need that time. Sometimes it's a male body, sometimes a female body.

We don't get into transmigration where we go back down the spiritual evolutionary scale to the animal or the mineral state. That's lifetimes and lifetimes past. But it also doesn't mean that this evolutionary scale goes straight up—or that it goes from plant to animal to human, where people can look down at their dog or cat and say, "Well, you are Soul, but I am a greater Soul because I am human. You still mess on the floor."

Some animals probably have a higher state of consciousness than their owners.

Some animals—I would say a great number of animals—probably have a higher state of consciousness than their owners.

People go to work. They become angry, they cheat if they can, and they indulge themselves in things that hurt both their physical body and other people who are dear to them. Then they come home, and the cat is always there, the dog is always there.

Treat your pets right, and they'll always love.

Treat your pets right, and they'll always love. They don't look at you with the eyes of judgment, saying, "You've got alcohol on your breath again." Cats and dogs won't do that to you. They'll love you even if you've just had Limburger cheese. They'll probably want some. "Just pet me, and let me sit in your lap," they say. "Be kind and good to me."

Cats and dogs are very nonjudgmental. And in this way, they're often superior to human beings.

We see somebody who is bumping the electric fence, a little bit out of the rhythm of life according to our idea of what the rhythm of life is, and we say, "This person is doing so-and-so. That person's head is sticking up about one head taller than everybody else in this social group." That is the social consciousness speaking. And we get very self-righteous about our opinions. We think we are always walking around in shining clothes and other people are always walking around in dirty rags. We are special.

Well, dogs and cats don't mind. Especially dogs. To dogs, their owners are always walking around in shining clothes, because they're always giving out food.

Misha's like that. Misha, the Siamese cat, is very loving, very open, very noble. But one time, the ECKist was going away, and she asked her niece to come over and feed her cat. The niece tells her friend, "I've got to feed Misha, and I'll be gone for awhile because Misha needs love. She needs her food, but she needs a lot more love. It's going to take a little while."

Her friend said, "Cats don't know the difference, they don't care. Just give her the food, and that's all she really cares about."

And the niece said, "Not *this* cat." Because that's how Misha was.

Misha and Lulu

The ECKist began to notice that there was a very close connection between the love that Misha gave and the behavior of a toy poodle she used to have named Lulu. Misha was acting a whole lot like Lulu.

Cats and dogs are very nonjudgmental. And in this way, they're often superior to human beings.

Lulu used to love to jump in her arms too. The woman would have to stoop just a little bit to let Lulu jump into her arms and soak up all the love. And Lulu used to have a blanket that she chewed holes in. The woman had stored it in the closet.

The woman wondered, *Has Lulu come back to me as Misha?*

One day, when the woman came home from work, she saw that the cat had gone through great pains to affirm this: that indeed Misha the kitty was once Lulu the dog. The cat had climbed into the closet and pulled out this big heavy blanket that the dog used to play with.

A Siamese cat is not quite as big as a toy poodle. Misha had pulled and dragged this thing out into the center of the room and then sat there. And so when the woman came home just thinking all this time, "Could Misha be Lulu come back?" the first thing she saw was the cat sitting on the blanket, speaking in the only language it knows, in the language of symbols. It was sitting on Lulu's old chewed-up blanket, sitting there with a smile on its face, saying, "Get it?"

Sometimes dancing to the rhythm of life just involves an understanding of your relationship with the Inner Master.

THE UPPER ROOM

Sometimes dancing to the rhythm of life just involves an understanding of your relationship with the Mahanta, the Living ECK Master—with the Inner Master.

An ECKist had a catering service out of her home, but she had always had this feeling that on the inner there was an upper room above her office. This was a strange image to have. But every time she prepared the food at home, she had this feeling about the upper room, and it frightened her. She didn't know why she was afraid of this upper room—which meant a higher state of consciousness. And it meant a little bit more too.

One day in contemplation, she decided that she would like to understand what this meant. What was all this about the upper room, and why was she so afraid of it? She shut her eyes and went into contemplation.

It was a big spacious room full of Light and Sound.

In contemplation she saw the Inner Master—the inner side of myself. Wah Z was dressed in white clothes, white shoes. And he said, "Come along. You want to go to the upper room?"

She was afraid, but the Master said, "Take my hand."

He took her hand, and they went up the stairs to the upper room. And she was afraid to go in. They came to the door. He opened it and said, "Would you like to go in?" She looked in.

It was a big spacious room full of Light and Sound. This is the Light and Sound of God, the Voice of God, the Holy Spirit. We know that the Holy Spirit appears as Light and Sound to those who are further along the spiritual path. People can see the Light as blue, green, pink, or white. Or they may hear a sound. It can be anything: a whistling tea kettle, the sound of a flute or violin, birds singing, the sound of a train off in the distance, the ringing of bells. These are actual sounds that people hear, sometimes during contemplation or during the day, as a background sound.

The Inner Master said, "Here's the upper room." It was spacious, well-lit; and there was strong but soft light and strong but soft music of God in the room. He took her into the room, and then they left.

Then they came back and did it again, the very same thing: went up the stairs, went into the room.

By showing her the upper room over and over, the Mahanta was asking her, "Are you willing to go into this higher state of consciousness? Are you willing to make a commitment to go into this higher state, this upper room?"

She had been afraid to because the human condition—or the human consciousness—is afraid to go outside of itself. And this is the value of Soul Travel.

Are you willing to go into this higher state of consciousness?

WHAT IS SOUL TRAVEL?

I don't know how to explain Soul Travel. I can't say it's that common in Eckankar, even though it was one of the foundations for the ECK teachings when Paul Twitchell brought them out in 1965.

Here's a way to understand it: The waking state right here is very much alive compared to the dream that you had last night. But those who have had a Soul Travel experience realize that the Soul Travel experience is that much more dynamic than just being aware here in the physical waking state.

Some of you know this. You've had a Soul Travel experience of one kind or another—where it is so clear, and you have such insight and perception of divine love that you cannot imagine it in your normal human state. And if you're fortunate enough to reach that, sometimes through the grace of your own inner unfoldment and the grace of the divine ECK and the Mahanta, you're very fortunate. You're very fortunate to have these Soul Travel experiences.

Some of you do. It takes persistence. You've got to stay with it. But more than persistence, it requires a pure heart, a pure and loving heart.

A Step Above

When the woman went to the room with the Inner Master for the third time, she realized something that hadn't occurred to her before: Just going to the room wasn't so important. Most important was accepting the fact that she was comfortable with a higher state of consciousness.

This is what was really important. And that she was comfortable with the Mahanta taking her to that upper room or to the higher state of consciousness.

This was a very vivid dream, which is a step above an ordinary dream. There are different degrees of consciousness and experiences that we recognize in ECK. And the higher they are, the more pure they will be. And the more pure they are, the simpler they become.

When you have a much higher dream, there are no symbols.

When you have a much higher dream, there are no symbols. You don't see rooms or anything of this nature. You just see Light or you hear Sound in the highest state, and you feel this immense amount of divine love.

There's nothing to compare to it. When you have this experience, changes will begin to occur in your life; you will turn a new leaf.

Helping ECK in a Quiet Way

For those of you who want to help with the missionary program of ECK in a quiet way, go to your local library and see if they have three of the Mahanta Transcripts books. There are many books in the series and more are coming.

Don't give every one of the Mahanta Transcripts to the library. Just give three different books to each library if the librarian will accept them. Coordinate this through your local ECK center. Give just three books because you're going to be spending your money for them. And if the librarian or somebody else decides not to put the books in the library, they may put them out on the discount table. All the money that you've spent to get the copies of the Mahanta Transcripts into a library will be out on a table for only a few people to find.

However, if the books are in the library—just three of them of this series—I think it will be very helpful for people. This way, you won't spend too much money and there will be enough information there for people who want to find out about the teachings of ECK and see if it suits them. They'll see if what they read in the books gives them the kind of spiritual help they're looking for. And if people want to know more about ECK, there are more books listed in the back of each book.

This way, we reach out to others to a point. We let people know about the teachings of ECK in public places, on TV, and in the public forum. But we don't go pounding on doors and pestering people, because that's not our way of doing missionary work. We like to respect the privacy, the individual space, and the beliefs of other people. If they have a religion that's working for them, leave them alone because they're exactly where they belong, the same as you.

We like to respect the privacy, the individual space, and the beliefs of other people.

BEING SENSITIVE TO OTHERS

It concerns me when ECK leaders use improper language and tell dirty jokes in public—when people know you're ECKists.

It hurts me because it hurts other people who may not be very firm on the path of ECK. They hear these people who have been in Eckankar for many years telling very off-color jokes to each other in loud voices in public places where other people may recognize them as ECKists. And they say, "Are these Higher Initiates? Is this what Eckankar is all about?" Remember that people are going to judge Eckankar first of all by you.

Now I don't have any objection to what you do at home or when people have no idea that you're connected with Eckankar. But going to an ECK seminar is like going to church. You don't go to church, sit in the back, and tell dirty jokes to each other while the minister's giving a sermon. If you are, and if that's all you're getting out of church, you belong in a different church, I'm afraid.

You have to be very sensitive, because you can knock someone else off the path when you're thoughtless.

The same is true in Eckankar. You have to be very sensitive, because you can knock someone else off the path when you're thoughtless and are not living up to your initiation level.

These things do happen and have happened at past seminars. You have to take responsibility for yourself. You're responsible not just for yourself but for the other person who is new on the path to God and is expecting the very most from those of you who are leaders.

This is why it's hard to be a true leader of anything; you have to live your principles. There's a saying that in an office you can fool your superiors but you can't fool those who are under you. And the same is true in Eckankar. You might be able to fool those who are above you in the local ECK area. But when other people who are just getting on the path overhear you telling very dirty jokes in public, they might decide there's nothing here for them if this is the highest and the best that Eckankar has to offer.

Eckankar has the highest teachings to offer.

And Eckankar has the highest teachings to offer.

Soul Travel gives you a glimpse of truth as a living, breathing part of you, so that you know something as truth.

But unfortunately sometimes people in ECK are not exercising their spiritual disciplines as they should and are not using right discrimination.

GLIMPSE OF TRUTH

An ECKist from London said that every time he does Soul Travel, it proves all his expectations are wrong. This is the thing about Soul Travel. It gives you such a glimpse of truth—not just as a piece of knowledge out there—but as a living, breathing part of you, so that you know something as truth.

Ironically, it also dashes your old expectations and beliefs to the ground. Often you find out that life is more beautiful and fuller than you had ever expected it to be. And God's creation is more wondrous.

Once you come to this realization, through Soul Travel or any other experience, you have a greater appreciation and respect for life and everything that's in it.

LIVING WATERS OF LIFE

One day in contemplation, the ECKist from London was walking down a mountain. It's a very steep mountain. As he gets about halfway down, he sees a little cave off to the side of the path. He goes into the cave, and there is the source of the stream that goes all the way down the mountain, joining up with other streams to become a river.

It's a hot, bright day. And the ECKist suddenly says, "I'm thirsty."

So he bends over at this little pool of water that's coming out of the rocks from the source. And he cups his hands together, puts them into the water, and brings them up to drink. But his hands go right through the water. He can't drink the water because his hands won't hold it. His hands are like ghost hands.

He wonders, *How am I going to drink this water?* He tries again and again. It doesn't work. "What shall I do?" he asks.

Suddenly he gets an idea. He says, "I come in the name of Sugmad." He cups his hands, and this time he's able to take some water in his hands and drink it. Then he says, "I come in the name of ECK," and again cups his hands. The water stays in his hands, and he takes another drink. Then he says, "I come in the name of the Mahanta." Again he scoops up the water and is able to drink it. His thirst is quenched now.

The ECKist wonders about this. Just then a little pebble comes rolling down the mountain slope.

He goes outside, and looks, and here's Wah Z, the Inner Master, coming down the mountain. Wah Z says, "I see you figured it out." And they talk about this water of life. Wah Z says, "Only those with a loving heart ever get to drink of the living water of life. Many may find it, but only those who come with love in their hearts will know what to give to drink of it."

It was a very nice lesson. The water of life, even as truth, appears to be available everywhere to everyone. But only those who know how to give love—or know what to give and how to give it—are able to drink of it, to receive truth.

GETTING TRUTH DIRECTLY

The teachings of ECK, these insights into how truth works, are also able to give you truth more directly. It doesn't come secondhand from me, sitting

The teachings of ECK, these insights into how truth works, are also able to give you truth more directly. It doesn't come secondhand.

You will find as you move forward on the path to God and unfold spiritually that you will become more filled with divine love.

on the stage talking to you. It comes directly through your own experiences.

You will find as you move forward on the path to God and unfold spiritually that you will become more filled with divine love, and you will have more kindness and compassion for other people. And in so doing, you will eventually become a Co-worker with God.

I'm grateful that you were all able to come here. I know that you will benefit spiritually. My love to you all on your journey home—on your journey home here, and on your journey home to God. May the blessings be.

ECK Summer Festival, Anaheim, California, Sunday, June 18, 1995

Do the best you can. Be the best you can. Because in trying to do and be the best, you are trying to express a quality of God.

10
THE SECRET OF LOVE

*W*e have cardinals in our yard at home. It always sounds to me as if one of their calls is "Phoebe." The bird books may call it something else, but to me when the cardinal gets up early in the morning, it always says, "Phoebe. Where's Phoebe?"

MORNING CALL

One morning two cardinals were outside. One would start out very, very softly and sweetly, "Phoebe?" No answer. "Phoebe." Still no answer. Then, "Phoebe!" It's 5:15 in the morning. And then he'd start all over again. "Phoebe?" He did this round of three calls for over half an hour. By then I was wide awake.

The sound struck me as funny. First it was very, very sweet just like a parent calling a child to breakfast. "Phoebe?" And Phoebe doesn't come or answer.

And then, "Phoebe." Now the parent's putting a little bit of elbow into it. And then more sternly, "Phoebe!" And still no answer. It's like the cardinal has this little tape that runs on a loop and knows only three tones.

Sometimes you see birds giving seed to each other.

They pick up a seed, walk over to another bird, and give the seed to the other bird. Especially in spring during mating season, they're very sweet to each other. I was thinking that sometimes the secret of love is shown in worlds other than the human world. Maybe birds — and animals too — show affection to each other that sometimes we humans are not aware of.

GOD'S LOVE FOR SOUL

One of the radio talk-show hosts is very into politics. When other people suggest that animals have feelings, he cannot listen to it. "Animals are animals," he believes. "What do you expect from animals?"

Those of you who have pets know that there is a bond of love between yourself and your pet. And the reason there is this bond of love is because you are Soul.

Most people don't realize that their pet is also Soul. Soul exists because God loves It. It's very simple. Soul exists because God loves It. And when two Souls set up a bond of love, it is stronger and more enduring than eternity. It doesn't matter if the two Souls are human beings or if one of them happens to be a bird, a dog, or a cat.

This would be shocking to most people who go to church on a Sunday morning. They'd hear this and say, "What? Animals and birds are Souls?" Notice that I don't say "have Souls" but "are Souls." Because Soul comes into the lower worlds and takes on a form according to Its state of consciousness.

YOUR PET'S UNCONDITIONAL LOVE

I have observed — and maybe you have too — that some pets seem to have a higher state of consciousness than some people. But when a pet shows love, consideration, and the quality of mercy, most people say, "Instinct."

A *Reader's Digest* article said that computers can do everything that people can do, but one thing that the writer had never been able to program into the computer was to enjoy what it was doing. And I thought, *So true*. When an animal does something that looks very human — showing compassion or love and mercy to its owner who is sick or feeling sorrow —that animal is far above computers in this sense. It is certainly far above some people because it can show and express God's love.

As people get older, sometimes they take in a pet, especially if they've lost a loved one. They find their dog gives them undying love. It's totally pure love.

You can't get this kind of love from other people, a love that's there no matter what you say or how bad you feel that day. But even if you say a few sharp words, the dog doesn't care, and certainly the cat doesn't—cats being the way they are.

PURPOSE OF LOVE

I'd like to read from *Stranger by the River* on the purpose of love. "God love has for its goal the creation of the highest form." And then it goes on, "and you must know that the individual love is likewise forever attempting to express itself in form, and to give Soul the highest architecture of spiritual attainment."

Do the best you can. Be the best you can. That's the bottom line. Because in trying to do and be the best, you are trying to express a quality of God, the divine nature. You're trying to be the highest it's possible to be.

But some people don't understand why they are

Do the best you can. Be the best you can.

here on earth. They wonder, *Is it to just put in my time until the final hour?* You've been saved, so what's there for you to do? Maybe you're here to live your faith. But if you don't live your faith, you still feel there's no harm done because you can just say in the eleventh hour, "I regret everything," and it's all OK. So you ask, Why waste my time living a very upright ethical life? Why bother?

In ECK, we know the reason to bother: It is that every minute counts. Every minute is an opportunity to develop the qualities of divine love and mercy.

And how do you do it? You start with the people who are closest to you. You show them warm love. To people in general, you give another kind of love, what the Bible calls charity. This is detached love. In other words, you have goodwill toward all people, but toward your loved ones—the ones who are close to you in your family—you give warm love.

You start with the people who are closest to you. You show them warm love.

UNDERSTANDING THE NATURE OF TRUTH

Rebazar Tarzs, the ECK Master, is talking to the seeker. "Open thine eyes, O man, and look steadily for love. Then you will learn the secrets as have I; the bright angel of the true Home will stand before you in a glorious robe. He will give you the secrets of love as never before imparted. But be cautious, my curious one, for it is dangerous to look for the angel of love unless you are filled with sincerity. He can blind you or make you great."

When I read this passage in *Stranger by the River* years ago, it was one of those nice excitements. I thought, *Oh, blind you or make you great. Well, I don't know about the first, but I sure would like to be spiritually great.*

But most people don't understand the nature of

truth. We think—at least before coming in contact with the teachings of ECK—that truth is always kind and gentle. That is an erroneous teaching. Truth is not always kind and gentle, nor is it easily understood or perceived by people.

Most people think, *I can tell a spade from a spade. I know truth when I hear it.* But the fact is, most people can't.

As an example: truth means not just hearing something that someone says to you and saying, "Oh, that is truth, that is wisdom." It's living it. If people know truth, they will live it. That means showing consideration for their family and friends, showing love and respect even when they're not feeling like it. Even saying thank you when we don't feel like saying thank you.

If people know truth, they will live it.

Guardian Angels and ECK Masters

Some people find the secret of love by a long meandering route. A woman from Mexico met one of the ECK Masters, Fubbi Quantz. These ECK Masters are the guardian angels we sometimes hear about today. ECK Masters *are* guardian angels, but not all guardian angels are ECK Masters. There's a difference.

A guardian angel's main function is to protect people. The guardian angel picks a person and stays with that one person, helps them out with whatever powers that guardian angel has.

A guardian angel's main function is to protect people.

But different angels have different powers in a hierarchy, the same way students in school are not all equal and alike. For instance, a first-grade student probably won't know as much math as a freshman in high school. Or a freshman in high school won't know as much grammar as a freshman in college.

"YOU WANT SPIRITUAL FREEDOM"

A woman was working in a store in Mexico City. It was a good store, and she liked the people she worked for. They sold valuable art, paintings, and old books. She was married, and she was going to have to be gone from work for forty-five days to travel to Europe with her husband. This also meant leaving her little girls. She was thinking that this trip would create some problems. She would have to give up her job, and her little girls would have to stay with relatives. So she really didn't want to go on this trip.

One day, near the time when she would have to leave, to give up her job, an old man came into the shop. He looked like he was from India, but he spoke only English.

One of the other people in the shop came up to her and said, "You speak English. So maybe you'd better help him."

The woman went up to him with a big smile on her face. As they talked, she was struck by the kindness of this gentleman. He was just so kind. And when he spoke, the words that came out of his mouth weren't just casual, ordinary words. They were words of wisdom. Everything was a golden gem.

The old man talked to her for quite a while. And then he said, "You're always smiling. But why are your eyes so sad?"

She said, "I think maybe it's because I don't have freedom inside myself. I have freedom out here, but I don't have it inside."

He said, "Ah, yes. Spiritual freedom. You want spiritual freedom."

She said, "I think maybe it's because I don't have freedom inside myself. I have freedom out here, but I don't have it inside."

THE SECRET OF LOVE

This was seven years before she'd learned about Eckankar. So she didn't know what he meant by spiritual freedom.

The old man pulled a coin out of his pocket and showed it to her. On the coin there was a face.

"Look carefully at the silver coin," the old man said. "See the face on it."

The woman looked at the face. "The person on the face of this coin is trying to lead people to spiritual freedom," the man told her. "I want you to have this coin."

"I can't just take your coin," she said.

He said, "Please, take the coin. It will always remind you of spiritual freedom."

Finally she took it, and she and her husband left for their trip to Europe soon after. They went to Spain, and they had a little time to go to Italy. When she was there, she had this feeling of déjà vu, that she had been in Italy before.

But she always wondered about the silver coin and what this old man had meant by spiritual freedom. And then seven years later she came across the teachings of ECK.

One time, she visited the ECK center and she saw drawings of the ECK Masters. One of them was of the ECK Master Fubbi Quantz, the gentleman she had met in the store. When she saw the drawing, she felt such love and gratitude that she had been given the secret of love—that she had found the teachings of ECK. This fountain of love had come into her life.

She had been looking for it her whole life. And until she had found the secret of love, knowing where to look for spiritual freedom, the sadness showed in her eyes. But now there was joy.

When she saw the drawing, she felt such love and gratitude that she had been given the secret of love—that she had found the teachings of ECK.

HEART AND MIND

A seeker on the East Coast of the United States was interested in one of the public classes that some of the ECKists were doing in her area. One was a class to discuss *The Dream Master,* one of the books of ECK. So she went to the class. She liked it.

After that, she attended a Soul Travel class — Soul Travel being one of the principles of the teachings of ECK. Soul Travel just means getting in touch with your higher nature, which is Soul. Soul Travel means moving from the human state of consciousness to the Soul state of consciousness.

One day, her fiancé said he would like to come along to the next dream class.

She hoped that he would like the class, because they were starting a relationship. They hoped to get married. She realized it's better if both of the couple have the same beliefs, because otherwise there can be problems. It's bad enough if one person in the couple has very tidy habits and the other doesn't. If one person in the relationship is very, very clean and the other one's definition of cleanliness is on another scale entirely — which means sloppy — then the couple is going to have problems with daily housekeeping. When do you do the dishes? And who does them? Are clothes picked up, hung in the closet?

Whenever you start a relationship, you think you know everything, heart-to-heart, about your mate. But soon it gets down to basic things like money, cleanliness, and children: How many? What kind? What's a good child? What's the way to raise them?

If you're going to a marriage counselor, instead of getting into your emotional differences, I think you should first look at basic habits. Does the person wash dishes? Clean up after himself? If you don't do these things, it doesn't matter if the other person does. But if you do, it *does* matter.

Then look at other down-to-earth aspects like spending money. Do you have the same idea of how and why to spend money? The woman may like to spend money on cookware and dresses because she feels it's important. A man may like to spend the money on tools or on investments that fail. But they've got to get along.

Otherwise, afterward you say to yourself, *Why didn't I think of this before I got into this mess?* But you don't have to go to a marriage counselor to uncover things like this.

The heart should speak louder than the mind when it comes to a relationship. But there is a balance between the two. Have heart, but don't lose your mind.

The heart should speak louder than the mind when it comes to a relationship. But there is a balance between the two.

ORANGE JUICE LESSON

So the seeker's fiancé went with her to one of the last meetings of the ECK classes on dreams. One day not long after, she was looking in the refrigerator. She was going to make a meal. And she said to herself, "I'd like some orange juice first."

There was one pitcher for juice in the refrigerator. She and her fiancé liked different brands, so they each had their own juice. But he was very kind, so he always mixed up her brand of frozen concentrate rather than his. She was very grateful that he didn't just make up his kind of juice and say, "Here." This particular day, she said, "Wait a minute. I've got another pitcher just like this. I'll make his kind for him and my kind for me. Clean out the refrigerator a little bit and there will be room for both pitchers." She mixed his juice in one pitcher and hers in the second one and put both pitchers in the refrigerator.

And then she realized what this meant. It was a message from Divine Spirit: you may have different beliefs, but if you clean things out of the refrigerator—out of the storage area of your heart—there'll be room enough for each of you. You can drink from your religion, and he can drink from his religion. There doesn't have to be a problem.

THERE'S ROOM FOR BOTH BELIEFS

Eckankar is a relatively new religious teaching, or spiritual path. Many people in ECK are married to Christians, atheists, agnostics, Hindus, or those from other religions, because we have people all around the world. And this big question often comes up: Can we each have our own religion?

You *can* get along. Just throw out some of your old beliefs, and there will be room for both of you side by side.

A man was telling me not long ago that when he and his wife were first dating, she was very open about his beliefs. When they got married, she suddenly became a born-again Christian.

When I was a Lutheran years ago, I knew there was nothing quite as strict as a born-again anything. It doesn't matter what. It can be in politics, a born-again Democrat or Republican. They're the worst kind.

This man and his wife had gotten along very nicely until she suddenly got religion. He said to her, "Why can't you follow your religion and let me follow mine? Love allows this kind of thing to its loved ones." She preached at him all the time.

If you love someone, you will love the person for what they are, and you can get along. But she kept

Just throw out some of your old beliefs, and there will be room for both of you side by side.

preaching at him, going on and on and on. They've separated, which always makes me feel very bad. I've gone through a divorce, and it's a hard time for everyone. Its not something you do lightly. It's not that anybody's at fault. It's just that you have your beliefs, and you have what you feel is important in life.

If there's any way possible to work it out, do. Clean out your refrigerator. Find what things you can throw out so that your pitchers can stand side by side.

WHEN THE LIGHT GOES OUT

A seeker in Germany went to the ECK center. She had noticed that there was something special about the ECKists at the ECK center. They were like shining lights. One woman was speaking, and around her a very bright, shining light was glowing.

A little while later, this seeker became a member of Eckankar. When she was in the ECK center she saw a notice on the bulletin board. It said that somebody wanted to sell some ECK books. She figured that one of the ECKists had probably died, or translated, and somebody was just getting rid of the person's books. The new ECKist thought, *This would be a good way to get some of the ECK books.*

She called the number, and a woman answered. "Come on over," the woman said. "Here's my address."

The new ECKist went over to the person's home, and when she got there, she found that the person who was selling the books was the woman whose face had been shining so brightly before. But now the new ECKist noticed that the glow was gone, the light was completely out. It struck her, and she wondered, *Doesn't this person know what she has lost?*

Most of the time when people lose a higher state

It struck her, and she wondered, Doesn't this person know what she has lost?

of consciousness, they don't know it. They've slipped out of this higher consciousness like water from a cup. The cup had been dipped into the spring of eternal life, the fountain of spiritual freedom, the fountain of love. A source of water that is precious beyond anything that you can imagine.

People often don't realize that they've lost something. They take a sip from the cup, or they drink a whole cup. They dip the cup into the fountain again, and they take some more water. Some people stay there and drink whenever they're thirsty. Other people just drink a sip or a cupful, and then they leave ECK.

We don't worry about it too much. A lot of people come, a lot of people go. But I'm happy to say more people stay every year. Otherwise I'd have to wonder, *Am I presenting the ECK teachings correctly? Are the ECK leaders presenting the ECK teachings correctly?*

We see the path of ECK not as something with four walls or a door that needs a lock.

OLD SOULS, YOUNG SOULS

We see the path of ECK not as something with four walls or a door that needs a lock. When people want to come into ECK, we say, "Certainly, come in." And when people want to leave, we say, "Blessings to you." And just leave it at that. Because we know they are Soul.

Whenever anyone's come into Eckankar and stayed, it's generally because they have come across the teachings of ECK in a past life before the teachings of ECK were known as Eckankar. They had made that connection.

Back then, they had their sip of water, and they tossed the rest of it away, saying, "I've had enough. It tastes bitter to my tongue. What is this? Truth? How can truth be bitter?"

Sometimes truth is bitter. Sometimes it's harsh. And sometimes for this reason we aren't able to recognize it. Because when we look at truth, we look at it through our state of consciousness—through our eyes, through our experience—not just from this lifetime but from every past lifetime. And the more experience we have, the more we are able to discern truth.

Some Souls that come to Eckankar are young Souls. They're the ones who take only the sip of water.

The ones who've been around a long time, long enough to realize that they've given up a blessing in the past by turning their back on the teachings of ECK, those are the ones who stay. They say, "I've turned my back on the secret of divine love once, twice, three times, hundreds of times before."

And each time it led to such sorrow, like the sorrow in the eyes of the woman in Mexico who was looking for spiritual freedom.

HOT DAY ON THE ROOF

Divine Spirit talks to us, sometimes in everyday events. We call it the Golden-tongued Wisdom, or the waking dream. The waking dream is when an event occurs that tells us something about our spiritual life.

So one weekend in June, an ECKist was home. It was a very hot day, and he was mowing the lawn and puttering around the garden. His next-door neighbor is a woman who sweeps her sidewalk twice a day—whether it needs it or not, she does it every day. He admits he isn't quite that strict about cleaning up the sidewalk. He'll shovel the walk in winter if it snows sometimes, but the rest of the time, who cares?

But this morning she called across to him when he was outside working on his yard. "You ought to

Divine Spirit talks to us, sometimes in everyday events.

take care of the ivy that's in your roof gutter," she said. "It's going to cause you a lot of problems later this summer, if you don't take care of it now."

He was walking around inside his house later and looked out of the upstairs window; he could see where the vine was climbing into the gutter. "That looks pretty easy to remove," the man said. "I'll just go down to the kitchen, get a knife, climb out on the roof, and cut it off. That will take care of the problem." Then he's done his good deed for the neighborhood.

As the man was ready to climb out on the roof, he hesitated. He's got these windows like guillotines. They've given him a couple of bruised knuckles. He would put the window up and be standing there with his hands on the windowsill looking around, and the window would suddenly come slamming down on his knuckles. He calls them his antiburglar devices.

So he had learned. He took a stick and very carefully propped the window open and climbed out on the roof. It was very hot out there. Very hot.

The vine was easy to take care of. It just came right out of the gutter. "That was easy," he said. He was ready to go back inside when suddenly he heard a dreadful sound. Somehow the stick had slipped out, and the window came crashing down and locked shut.

So now he's locked out on the roof.

But he's not worried. He'll just wait until the neighbor woman comes out or somebody comes home, and then he'll call down and say, "Hey, how about opening the window so I can get back inside?"

But nobody comes. The neighbor lady has been outside all morning but now she was nowhere in sight. And he's up there. He sits down and waits and waits. But it's getting hotter. The sun is really beating down on him, and the roof and his hands are

Somehow the stick had slipped out, and the window came crashing down and locked shut.

burning because the asphalt shingles are very, very hot. The tar is melting underneath them.

Now he's getting kind of concerned. *It's only a fifteen foot jump off the roof,* he thinks. *I could do that.* But he'd also noted that in cases just like this his family has a history of accidents where they break their ankles.

WAKING DREAM INSIGHTS

So he's sitting there thinking and thinking, and finally it occurs to him. He says, "I'll ask the Inner Master."

"Mahanta," he says, "what should I do?" Nothing happened.

So he says, "Maybe I have to look at my situation as a waking dream. OK, I'm way up here on the roof. That's like being in the Soul body, cut off completely from the world," which he was. And he says, "The stick is my ego. Prop it up, put it in place to open the window between myself and God. But you can't trust the ego. That thing always slips at the least opportune time. You're making some spiritual progress. Then you get angry or vain about something, lose your temper, and the window comes down."

"And you can't count on your neighbors," he says. Because he's up on the roof, that means anybody lower on the ground is of the lower consciousness. He says, "You can't count on the lower state of human consciousness," as opposed to the spiritual or Soul consciousness.

You can't count on the lower state of human consciousness.

So he waits. Again he asks, "Mahanta, what shall I do?" And he gets the feeling that maybe he should go ahead and jump. He gets to the edge of the roof, sticks his legs over the edge, and is about ready to jump. And the feeling goes away. He's puzzled. He says, "Well, if not jump, then what? Maybe I should look for help one more time."

So he gets up, backs away from the edge, walks around the roof, and sees the mail carrier in front of the house.

"Can you help me down?" he calls. "I seem to be stuck on the roof."

And the mail carrier says, "Oh, really? I thought that just happened to me."

He gives the mail carrier directions to find a ladder in the garage. She brings it around and sets it up. She guides his foot on to the first rung of the ladder. Finally he gets down.

The man's getting an insight into his spiritual condition. The window is actually the window of Soul.

Then he realizes that the mail carrier is someone who travels from house to house—like a spiritual traveler. The ECK Masters—the guardian angels—are spiritual travelers. They move around both in the physical and the other worlds to give help and comfort to people who need it.

The man's getting an insight into his spiritual condition. The window is actually the window of Soul. Ego gets in the way and prevents him from getting into his home which is God. It takes a spiritual traveler to help him—by putting a ladder up where he's stranded and helping him get back to earth. Then he can go forward with his spiritual life.

CHOOSING TO STAY

A woman in Little Rock, Arkansas, was critically ill over the winter. There were holes in her stomach from an infection. The doctors had tried everything. They had put in tubes to drain off the infection. But nothing was working. Finally the specialist gave up hope. He said, "I just don't know what else to do."

The woman would get very high fevers. And

when the fevers got high, she hovered at the point
of leaving this life.

After a few days the doctor said, "We've decided
to change the tubing. It will mean another operation."

They took her into the operating room, and they
were working on her. Suddenly she was outside her
physical body, looking down from the Soul viewpoint.
Those of you who are in ECK know this is an example
of Soul Travel. In this higher state of consciousness,
the woman saw the doctors working over her.

Suddenly the line on the heart monitor went flat.
It meant that her heart had stopped. But here she
is watching the whole thing. She sees her body on
the operating table. The doctor's trying everything
to bring her back to life. But she's there.

The woman notices the Inner Master, Wah Z,
beside her, and she takes his hand. She says to him,
"Do I go or do I stay?"

She looked in his eyes and saw unconditional
love. It was her choice. She had a choice of whether
to stay with her body, which had given her so much
pain through the winter, or go and be free. She decided
to stay because she wanted to be with her family.
Instantly she was back. She opened her eyes and
looked into the face of the specialist who's operating
on her. He was very, very concerned.

The next day he said to her, "Thank God the new
antibiotic we tried worked. It got you back just in the
nick of time."

LIVE JOYFULLY

But the ECKist knew what really had happened.
She knew that the Spiritual Traveler—the Mahanta,
the Inner Master—had been with her. The name of

Suddenly she was outside her physical body, looking down from the Soul viewpoint.

this individual is Wah Z. It's the inner side of myself.

She realized that life is something to live joyfully. Live it joyfully because you're learning to be a Co-worker with God.

This means practice the God qualities even on the days you don't feel like practicing the God qualities. These are the times it's really hard to practice your spiritual disciplines.

BECOME A MAGNET OF LOVE

If you desire love, try to realize that the only way to get love is by giving love.

In the chapter of *Stranger by the River* titled "Love" Rebazar Tarzs says, "Therefore, if you desire love, try to realize that the only way to get love is by giving love. That the more you give, the more you get; and the only way in which you can give is to fill yourself with it, until you become a magnet of love."

Here is the secret of love, this divine secret. Rebazar says to the seeker: "All things will gravitate to thee if ye will let love enter thine own hearts, without compromise."

That is the secret of love.

*ECK Worship Service, Temple of ECK,
Chanhassen, Minnesota, Sunday, August 6, 1995*

Glossary

Words set in SMALL CAPS are defined elsewhere in this glossary.

ARAHATA.   An experienced and qualified teacher for ECKANKAR classes.

CHELA.   A spiritual student.

ECK.   The Life Force, the Holy Spirit, or Audible Life Current which sustains all life.

ECKANKAR.   Religion of the Light and Sound of God. Also known as the Ancient Science of SOUL TRAVEL. A truly spiritual religion for the individual in modern times, known as the secret path to God via dreams and SOUL TRAVEL. The teachings provide a framework for anyone to explore their own spiritual experiences. Established by Paul Twitchell, the modern-day founder, in 1965.

ECK MASTERS.   Spiritual Masters who can assist and protect people in their spiritual studies and travels. The ECK Masters are from a long line of God-Realized SOULS who know the responsibility that goes with spiritual freedom.

HU.   The most ancient, secret name for God. The singing of the word HU, pronounced like the word *hue,* is considered a love song to God. It is sung in the ECK Worship Service.

INITIATION.   Earned by the ECK member through spiritual unfoldment and service to God. The initiation is a private ceremony in which the individual is linked to the Sound and Light of God.

LIVING ECK MASTER.   The title of the spiritual leader of ECKANKAR. His duty is to lead SOULS back to God. The Living ECK Master can assist spiritual students physically as the Outer Master, in the dream state as the Dream Master, and in the spiritual worlds as the

Inner Master. Sri Harold Klemp became the MAHANTA, the Living ECK Master in 1981.

MAHANTA.   A title to describe the highest state of God Consciousness on earth, often embodied in the LIVING ECK MASTER. He is the Living Word.

PLANES.   The levels of heaven, such as the Astral, Causal, Mental, Etheric, and Soul Planes.

SATSANG.   A class in which students of ECK study a monthly lesson from ECKANKAR.

THE SHARIYAT-KI-SUGMAD.   The sacred scriptures of ECKANKAR. The scriptures are comprised of twelve volumes in the spiritual worlds. The first two were transcribed from the inner PLANES by Paul Twitchell, modern-day founder of ECKANKAR.

SOUL.   The True Self. The inner, most sacred part of each person. Soul exists before birth and lives on after the death of the physical body. As a spark of God, Soul can see, know, and perceive all things. It is the creative center of Its own world.

SOUL TRAVEL.   The expansion of consciousness. The ability of SOUL to transcend the physical body and travel into the spiritual worlds of God. Soul Travel is taught only by the LIVING ECK MASTER. It helps people unfold spiritually and can provide proof of the existence of God and life after death.

SOUND AND LIGHT OF ECK.   The Holy Spirit. The two aspects through which God appears in the lower worlds. People can experience them by looking and listening within themselves and through SOUL TRAVEL.

SPIRITUAL EXERCISES OF ECK.   The daily practice of certain techniques to get us in touch with the Light and Sound of God.

SUGMAD.   A sacred name for God. Sugmad is neither masculine nor feminine; It is the source of all life.

WAH Z.   The spiritual name of Sri Harold Klemp. It means the Secret Doctrine. It is his name in the spiritual worlds.

INDEX

Introductory Books on Eckankar

The Slow Burning Love of God
Mahanta Transcripts, Book 13
Harold Klemp

What happens to those first bright flames of your most profound spiritual experiences? You know what you've found is real, but as the intensity fades you wonder. Learn to keep the bright flames of God's slow burning love alive in your heart. Experience the presence of God in your life. See truth when it comes to you, solve problems, and find your next spiritual step.

ECKANKAR—Ancient Wisdom for Today

Are you one of the millions who have heard God speak through a profound spiritual experience? This introductory book will show you how dreams, Soul Travel, and experiences with past lives are ways God speaks to you. An entertaining, easy-to-read approach to Eckankar. Reading this little book can give you new perspectives on your spiritual life.

Ask the Master, Book 1
Harold Klemp

"What is my purpose in life?" "Are dreams real?" "How do past lives affect us today?" Harold Klemp, the spiritual leader of Eckankar, gives clear and candid answers to these and other questions he receives from people around the globe. His answers can help you overcome fear, learn self-discipline, be more creative, and improve family relationships.

HU: A Love Song to God
(Audiocassette)

Learn how to sing an ancient name for God, HU (pronounced like the word *hue*). A wonderful introduction to Eckankar, this two-tape set is designed to help listeners of any religious or philosophical background benefit from the gifts of the Holy Spirit. It includes an explanation of the HU, stories about how Divine Spirit works in daily life, and exercises to uplift you spiritually.

For fastest service, phone (612) 544-0066 weekdays between 8 a.m. and 5 p.m., central time, to request books using your credit card. Or write: **ECKANKAR, Att: Information, P.O. Box 27300, Minneapolis, MN 55427 U.S.A.**

There May Be an
Eckankar Study Group near You

Eckankar offers a variety of local and international activities for the spiritual seeker. With hundreds of study groups worldwide, Eckankar is near you! Many areas have Eckankar centers where you can browse through the books in a quiet, unpressured environment, talk with others who share an interest in this ancient teaching, and attend beginning discussion classes on how to gain the attributes of Soul: wisdom, power, love, and freedom.

Around the world, Eckankar study groups offer special one-day or weekend seminars on the basic teachings of Eckankar. Check your phone book under **ECKANKAR**, or call **(612) 544-0066** for membership information and the location of the Eckankar center or study group nearest you. Or write **ECKANKAR, Att: Information, P.O. Box 27300, Minneapolis, MN 55427 U.S.A.**

☐ Please send me information on the nearest Eckankar center or study group in my area.

☐ Please send me more information about membership in Eckankar, which includes a twelve-month spiritual study.

Please type or print clearly   940

Name _____
          first (given)   last (family)

Street_____ Apt. # _____

City _____ State/Prov. _____

ZIP/Postal Code _____ Country _____

About the Author

Sri Harold Klemp was born in Wisconsin and grew up on a small farm. He attended a two-room country schoolhouse before going to high school at a religious boarding school in Milwaukee, Wisconsin.

After preministerial college in Milwaukee and Fort Wayne, Indiana, he enlisted in the U.S. Air Force. There he trained as a language specialist at the University of Indiana and a radio intercept operator at Goodfellow AFB, Texas. Then followed a two-year stint in Japan where he first encountered Eckankar.

In October 1981, he became the spiritual leader of Eckankar, Religion of the Light and Sound of God. His full title is Sri Harold Klemp, the Mahanta, the Living ECK Master. As the Living ECK Master, Harold Klemp is responsible for the continued evolution of the Eckankar teachings.

His mission is to help people find their way back to God in this life. Harold Klemp travels to ECK seminars in North America, Europe, and the South Pacific. He has also visited Africa and many countries throughout the world, meeting with spiritual seekers and giving inspirational talks. There are many videocassettes and audiocassettes of his public talks available.

In his talks and writings, Harold Klemp's sense of humor and practical approach to spirituality have helped many people around the world find truth in their lives and greater inner freedom, wisdom, and love.

International Who's Who of Intellectuals
Ninth Edition

Reprinted with permission of Melrose Press Ltd., Cambridge, England, excerpted from *International Who's Who of Intellectuals, Ninth Edition,* Copyright 1992 by Melrose Press Ltd.